Unspoken
Abandonment

by
Bryan A. Wood

ISBN: 1466315946
ISBN-13: 978-1466315945

Cover (rear) photograph credit: by Jessica Charles Photography, Saint Petersburg, Florida.

For ordering, contact, or additional information about the author, visit:

www.BryanWoodBooks.com

"*Life is full of influences, it's your application that sets you apart. That's something I wrote to myself and completely believe in. You can't be scared to set out to do something in life because you believe it may be similar to something, or because you don't know the clear cut path on how you're going to accomplish your goal or dream! Just take a step towards your belief daily — fearlessly, wholeheartedly, digging and dreaming within yourself, believing that as you push on through sacrifice, you will one day stand alone on top of a hill that you created that now encourages and inspires others to chase their dream. Knowing that through tenacity and patience anything can be achieved. If you simply believe.*"

-Charles "Mask" Lewis

"*Far better it is to dare mighty things, to win glorious triumphs even though checkered by failure, than to rank with those poor spirits who neither enjoy nor suffer much because they live in the gray twilight that knows neither victory nor defeat.*"

-Theodore Roosevelt

CONTENTS

Acknowledgments

January 24, 2011 is a day that will be a part of me forever. Sergeant Thomas Baitinger and K9 Officer Jeffery Yazlowitz, you will always be in my heart, and you will never be forgotten. Tom, you will forever be my friend and my hero.

I would never be where I am today without the love and support of my wonderful parents. They have enjoyed me at the best of times, stayed beside me during the worst of times, and let me find my own way when I needed it the most. I will forever be in their debt.

To my wonderful Abier: I love you, and you make my sun shine on even the cloudiest day. You are everything to me, and you are always there for me when I need you the most. You are my world.

1

On Patrol

THE SKY IS A brilliant shade of blue, without the trace of a single cloud. I am just sitting back in the late afternoon sun, and I am relaxing as I feel its rays gently warm my face. The cooling breeze prevents me from becoming too warm, and the moment is perfect. I look up and see an even more beautiful sight.

I cannot see her features, only her profile cast by the sun as it slowly dips towards the horizon. Her long, chestnut-brown hair flows behind her as she playfully chases the young child in front of her. She looks towards me and offers a smile that still melts me to my soul. She stops playing with the child and stares at me for a moment. Running her fingers through her hair, she looks at me in a way that any other man would envy; it was a look of complete love.

"Mommy, keep playing!" the child cries out. The young five-year-old girl then looks to me and asks, "Daddy, are you going to play now?"

Without a response, I get up and run towards her. I grab her in my arms as she leaps up at me. She says, "Daddy, it's coming loose again. Will you fix it for me?"

I carry her to a nearby picnic table and set her down. That is when this feeling struck me; I am happy. I am truly, honestly, and completely happy. Sure, I wish I had more money, I wish that all weekends were three days long, and I still want a bigger television; however, what I have, right here and right now, is a complete and absolute peace of mind.

It was not always this way. I will come back to this moment and pick up right here again, but before I do, there is something I need to explain. I was once very far from where I am today. There was a part of me which had been taken, and I feared it was gone forever. It has been a long and difficult journey for me, but I am every bit the stronger for having endured it.

I remember a time in life when I felt like I could conquer the world. I felt as though I was unstoppable. The truth, however, is that I was just a naïve kid that didn't know his ass from his elbow, but at the time, I honestly thought I had it all figured out. I was fun, quick-witted, and I had a brilliant smile and blue eyes that have earned me compliments my entire life. I had seen neither poverty nor suffering in my life, though I thought I had, but I soon would.

Life is very easy for some and very difficult for others. Regardless of which side you fall on, one thing is for certain: you will face challenges in your life, and it is how you face and overcome these challenges that will ultimately define you as a person. What I am about to share is the story of my greatest challenge.

• • •

I am not exactly sure where to begin, so I will start on a balmy, summer night in central Florida. The sun had already gone down, but the temperature was still above ninety degrees. I was driving, with the windows opened, feeling the summer air blow in and hearing the sounds of a busy city street. The car in front of me was an older model, maroon four-door, and I had been following it for a few minutes. I saw the car blow right through the red light as it was turning northbound on 102nd Street from Lexington Avenue. I figured that this was the safest place to stop the vehicle, so I reached up, turned on my over head lights, and hit the siren for a few short blasts. The car started to pull to the side of the road, and I reached for my microphone.

"Four Six Lima, going out on a traffic stop," I said with a sense of certainty into the microphone.

The dispatcher responded quickly, "Four Six Lima, go ahead."

"It's going to be a Florida license plate, on an older maroon sedan, and we will be in front of the car wash on 102nd."

"The car wash on 102nd, ten-four. Request a second unit?" the dispatcher asked.

"No, I'm fine."

My right hand was resting cautiously on the grip of my gun as I approached the driver. I was walking very slowly, struggling to see through the dark tinted windows, and I was hoping for a glimpse of who was inside the car. As I arrived at the driver's window, the tinted glass came down, and I could see a middle-aged woman alone in the vehicle. I did not see anything unusual or suspicious, so I asked the driver for her license and registration.

She nervously asked, "Did I do something wrong, sir?"

"As soon as I have your driver's license and registration, I will explain everything to you."

She kindly obliged, and I told her, "When you were traveling eastbound on Lexington Avenue and made the turn onto 102nd Street, you went right through that red light. Try to relax for a few minutes, and I'll have you on your way. I do like that you're wearing your seatbelt, so if everything checks out, I don't think there will be a need for a ticket."

I began walking back to my car, and as the blue strobe lights were flashing in my face, I could feel a strange sensation coming over me. It was not the first time; in fact, it had happened several times before. The prior occurrences gave me a warning of what was to come next. I turned back to the vehicle and gave the driver her license and registration.

"Here you are ma'am. You're free to go." I quickly said.

As I felt myself beginning to sweat, I hurried back to my police cruiser with each breath becoming more rapid. I drove into the nearest parking lot, and I began to have my latest panic attack.

I sat alone in my police car with the windows rolled up and the air conditioning on the maximum setting. I had a feeling of fear and terror rushing through my body as I struggled for air. A simple breath was not so simple anymore. The feeling lasted for only a short time, but it seemed to last forever.

After a few minutes, I was able to regain my composure. I was drenched in sweat, and I tried to relax for a moment as I worked to collect my thoughts. I reflected on the incident, and it made no sense to me. I was not scared during the traffic stop, I was not threatened in the least by the driver, and it is something I routinely do every day. So, why today, why right now, and why all the other times this has happened before?

The attack eventually ended, and I went back about my night handling the random calls that came in and doing the occasional traffic stop. The remainder of that shift was uneventful and otherwise unremarkable.

After my shift, I turned in my police cruiser and walked to my personal vehicle. During the thirty-five minute drive home, I repeatedly thought about the panic attack from earlier in my shift. I knew it was nothing which I could control, but it made me feel like I was either weak or as though there was something wrong with me. I knew then, as I still do now, that those ideas were not true, but it was a difficult feeling to shake.

I arrived home just a little past one-thirty in the morning. I opened the refrigerator, hoping to find dinner, but there was nothing prepared. I very rarely came home to a cooked meal; instead, it was usually a frozen dinner or a drive-through on the way from work. I had a quick snack, I took a shower, and then I slid into bed absolutely exhausted.

I tried desperately to sleep that night, but I just couldn't. I had already experienced multiple panic attacks by that point in time, but that most recent one was really bothering me.

The attacks occurred very infrequently in the beginning, maybe once a month or less. Eventually, they progressed to what seemed like a once per week event. They were always set off for no apparent reason; they just appeared.

"Why is this happening to me? Why me?" I asked myself so many times.

Panic attacks were not my only worry. I was going to work and walking through life pretending that I was fine. I worked hard not to show the truth, and I honestly thought no one could see what was just beneath my surface. I looked to everyone around me, praying that someone would see the truth and call me out on it. However, I did too well of a job pretending to be whole, even when I knew I was being torn to pieces on the inside.

It was about four o'clock in the morning, and I still could not sleep. Like so many other nights, I was laying awake and looking at the ceiling. My eyes had adjusted to the dark, and I was watching the ceiling fan, almost hypnotized by its repetitive movement. This position was nothing new to me, and I decided to take one of the pills my doctor had prescribed to help me sleep.

I made my way to the kitchen and opened the medicine bottle, dropping two pills into the damp palm of my hand. I sat for a minute or two and just stared at the pills. My mind was racing off in its own direction. I do not know if it was anxiety, frustration, or something else that hit me at that moment, but I realized I had had enough. I was not going to live like this anymore, and this needed to stop. This was the very moment I decided to take control and get my life back. It was an epiphanic moment which I will never forget.

I had recently had a talk with a friend who had given me what would ultimately be the advice I needed to move forward, and it was the advice I needed to put this portion of my life behind me for good. I had been given this almost-magical advice, but I had no idea how to even begin to use it. At that very moment, as I stared at those two pills, the answer came to me, and I knew exactly where to begin.

I walked from my kitchen to the garage, and I flipped a switch, bringing life to the flickering overhead, fluorescent light. The garage was nearly silent with the gentle hum of the light's power supply being the only sound.

Sitting in the corner, under a pile of typical garage clutter, was a very plain, nondescript, black footlocker. There was no padlock on it or anything to identify what was inside; however, as I looked at it I knew that within this box was the heart of my fears. I had not opened the box once since I packed it three years earlier. I packed its contents and closed it, for what I thought would be forever. It turned out that it would not be forever, and the time had come to open it once again.

I dragged the footlocker to the center of the garage, and I knelt down next to it. My hands trembled as I slowly unclasped the latches and began to open the creaking lid.

As I opened the box, I could instantly smell an odor that I had all but forgotten. It was a ripe smell that is nearly impossible to describe: a mixture of pollution, filth, and garbage. I found it amazing that, even after three years, the interior still smelled like the air so many thousands of miles away. I have since shown the footlocker to others, but no one else can detect the odor I smell when I see the contents inside. It still does not make sense to me how I can smell something no one else can, merely by looking at the contents inside of an old box.

The box was littered with random trinkets and war mementos. I barely remembered packing any of this at all. How could all of this have faded from my memory? I began rifling through the contents and found a tattered burqa, Afghan money, and other odd items. I was wondering why I even bothered to save this stuff, when suddenly, I saw something that instantly caused my heart to skip a beat and fall into the pit of my stomach. I found exactly what I was looking for; it was a simple, black and white, hard-covered composition notebook with the single word "Journal" handwritten on the cover. This was the journal I had kept while I was in Afghanistan.

I removed the journal from the footlocker and held it in my hands. Part of me wanted to throw the book back into the footlocker and let it stay there, but I knew that in order for me to take the first step toward putting my life back together, I needed to open that book and read every word sandwiched between its cardboard cover. The latter thought won the struggle, and a knot developed in my throat as I opened the cover and began to read the first page.

I sat on the cold cement floor of my garage, reading the journal that felt like it had been written a lifetime ago. The night passed by as I read, and the morning's rising sun brought with it a life changing journey. I want to share with you that journey and how I arrived at that moment, and it all begins with that journal.

● ● ●

Bryan A. Wood

2

The Journal

JUST A DAY OR two before I left for Afghanistan, I visited a local supermarket to get some items I thought I may need over the coming weeks. I decided to stock up on toothbrushes, deodorant, toothpaste, and other such products to get me through the days until my first care packages would begin arriving. I also got some comfort items, such as candy and magazines, to make the same period of time more tolerable.

I was in the stationary section, looking for paper and envelopes to use for writing letters, when I saw a black and white composition notebook. I knew I was embarking on something incredible, and as I saw that notebook I thought to myself, "Wouldn't that be something to keep a running journal to remember this adventure forever?"

I purchased the notebook, and I did write just such a journal. However, what started out as something to be remembered forever eventually became something I could never forget. Here is my journal, word for word, exactly as it was originally written:

February 22, 2003:

We were on the plane coming into Bagram, Afghanistan, when the pilot announced we were fifteen minutes out. Thirteen hours earlier, we were yelling and excited, but now not a single word was being spoken on the same plane. I initially thought everyone around me was simply tired, even though I was wide awake. We were in the back of a C-17 transport plane, with our seatbacks against the wall, and I could see everyone else was awake also. Although no one mentioned it, I think we were all very afraid. We were afraid of the known and even more afraid of the unknown. All of our briefings to this point told us we were just minutes away from stepping foot in a country filled with landmines, a hostile and motivated enemy, an unwelcoming civilian population, and a long uphill battle. All I could think was, "Holy shit, what have I gotten myself into?"

The plane landed fine, but the landing was very unique. All of the lights were turned off on the aircraft, and even the runway was blacked out with no lights at all. A sniper only needs to see the slightest movement to identify you as a target, and the only advantage we would have on a wide open airfield would be to remain under the cover of darkness. The pitch black night was somewhat comforting in that aspect.

After offloading from the plane, we each had to carry all of our gear and equipment by hand as we were led off in a single file line. We walked for a little more than a mile, in complete silence and darkness, until we reached Bagram's temporary barracks. We were told to drop our gear, pick a rack, and get some sleep. The room was cold, dirty, and had a horrible stench. The "bed" was little more than a thin foam mat laid over a piece of plywood on the floor. I already wanted to go home, but I know I have a job to do first. Despite the cold, the smell, and the discomfort, I fell asleep faster than I ever have before.

February 23, 2003:

We got our wakeup at approximately five o'clock in the morning, local time. We hadn't hit our racks more than four hours earlier, so it was not exactly a great night's sleep. After we ate breakfast, we were all guided to another area of Bagram Air Base. This was my first look at Afghanistan.

It was a beautiful day, but the area was very dirty, old, and quite worn. The buildings on the base were battered and showed the signs of years of war. We were instructed to stay on the roadways because of the incredibly high number of landmines left behind by the Soviets during their withdrawal from the country. We were told the landmines were very old and deteriorated but still had the ability to kill and seriously maim. My legs have done well by me so far in life, and I intend to hang on to them just a little longer.

After breakfast, I still had no idea where I was going or what I would be doing in Afghanistan. My unit was told essentially nothing. It was broad daylight, but we were still in the dark. All of the gear we had carried off from the plane was still stored in the temporary barrack from the previous night. We were instructed to gather up our gear and be ready for transport trucks which were en route to get us. Once we got to the barrack, two 5-ton trucks were waiting for us. We loaded our gear into the back, and then we stood by waiting for our "security escort."

I think we waited for an hour or so until our escort finally arrived. The escort consisted of six heavily armored HUMVEE trucks, each with either a fifty caliber machine gun or fully automatic grenade launcher in the turret. I knew this could not be a good sign.

As the HUMVEEs stopped, the rear door of one opened up, and my old friend, Sean, came running towards me from within the truck. I knew my unit was coming to replace his, and I knew he was in country, but I never expected to run into him so soon. Sean ran to me and nearly tackled me to the ground in excitement. He has been here for six months and since my unit is his relief, he is going home. I asked Sean where we were going and what it was like. Sean described a small compound in the middle of downtown Kabul. He told me it was a very small area, in the heart of the city. Sean told me, "Dude, this place is really fucked up."

My squad, along with one other squad, loaded up in the back of one of the 5-ton trucks. The rear of the truck was covered with a canvas tarp and had no doors or windows. If we could see out then anyone else could see in, and we would be sitting ducks. The hour-long ride from Bagram to Kabul was long, dark, bumpy, and boring. Anxiety was starting to fade into exhaustion, and I really just wanted to sleep more than anything else.

We arrived to a military compound in the heart of Kabul. The compound, called Camp Eagle, was very small at only about the size of a city block. The walls of the compound are right next to the city's streets, and there are people everywhere outside of the walls. We were told our primary duties will be to accomplish tasked missions and provide safety and security for the compound's operations against any and all threats. Recent threats to Camp Eagle include rocket attacks and a suicide bomber who used a pair of hand grenades to kill one Afghan local and two American Special Forces soldiers. One of the guys welcoming us said, "Have fun guys. Protecting this place is like trying to protect a virgin on prom night. Eventually someone is going to get through."

The housing in Camp Eagle is actually relatively nice, and I use "relatively" very strongly. The building in which we will be living was once the Japanese embassy. We have running water, showers, and indoor plumbing. There is no heat and although it may be cold for now, winter will be over soon. The entire squad is assigned to one room in the basement. While nine guys in one small room may seem bad, it is a lot better than living in a tent back at Bagram.

There are a lot of Afghan civilians working inside of Camp Eagle. It is kind of unsettling to see so many civilian locals inside the walls of the compound, and it is very apparent most of them do not seem to like us. There are Afghan groundskeepers, translators, construction workers, and laborers. They are everywhere.

The day was filled with getting our gear sorted and getting ourselves settled in. Bed time came quickly, and by the time it had I was completely drained. It is bitter cold in here, but I am so tired I think I'll barely notice as I fall asleep. Today was a very long day.

February 24, 2003:

We woke up to another early start today. I went upstairs to the kitchen area and I was shocked to see Afghans making our food. I was told every Afghan civilian on the compound has had a background clearance done, but I am still a little uneasy with eating food made by them. Everyone who has been in the compound for a while tells me they have more than earned our trust, but I really have no choice but to eat it. As much as I hate to admit this, it was actually pretty good.

Right after breakfast, the squad was told to be ready in fifteen minutes for our first tour of downtown Kabul. We left Camp Eagle in a line of HUMVEEs and I was the machine gunner in the second vehicle. The vehicle has a large circular hole in the roof, called a turret, with a machine gun mount. As we rolled beyond the safety of the gates and into the city, I sat perched out of the turret with my M249 machinegun locked and loaded. I had sat in that same position countless times in training, but never in a hostile environment. I have never felt as vulnerable in my entire life as I did being so exposed in that turret.

Leaving Camp Eagle and riding into Kabul was an instant culture shock. The Taliban may no longer control Kabul, but it is absolutely still a war zone. Every other building is either riddled with bullet holes or gaping holes from various explosions. People are armed everywhere. Civilians are just walking down the street with AK47s and SKS rifles. I saw one child, no older than thirteen or fourteen carrying an assault rifle.

The streets are also disgustingly filthy. We passed down one narrow roadway where I saw a man in his thirties or forties taking a shit on the side of the road. One of the experienced troops that we are replacing was riding in the vehicle with us. Over the loud interior noise of the HUMVEE he explains that standards are very different in Kabul and, although not encouraged, this kind of behavior is not uncommon.

The tour continued on for approximately an hour with nothing eventful being seen except the magnitude of extreme poverty. That is when we stumbled upon a woman being beaten by two men. The woman, wearing a dark blue Burqa, was on her knees and struggling to stand, as one man beat her with a belt and the other pushed her back to the ground. As we drove by this scene, our "guide" told us this was very common in Kabul, and he said, "Try not to let it bother you." He told us we were going to see a lot of things that would bother us here, but we cannot get involved in this kind of mess. You just have to look the other way.

The women here all wear a blue Burqa. The Burqa is a long robe, which covers the woman from head to ankle. Over the face is a layer of mesh cloth that enables the woman to see out but allows no one to see her. It is a very strange feeling seeing a person wearing this type of thing. Every woman here is wearing one, and there are no exceptions.

The squad returned to Camp Eagle and had a lot of briefings. I found out my squad would be assigned to the midnight to eight o'clock in the morning shift for perimeter security. During the day we will be assigned to various missions outside of the compound as they are assigned. We were told we will be working seven days a week with no days off, but I guess you really do not need a day off here; it's not like there is anything fun to do. I went to bed after dinner for a quick nap before starting my first midnight shift.

February 25, 2003:

I showed up at the front gate of the compound just a few minutes before midnight. I was greeted by the guy I was relieving with a sarcastic "Have fun."

A non-English speaking Afghan guard walked up to me and placed his fisted hand over his heart while he said, "Salom."

I extended my right hand, and he shook it eagerly with a large smile on his face. I could not understand a word he was saying, but it was obvious he was happy to meet me.

There are several Afghan guards which patrol the outer layers of the compound. These guards are not very professional looking at all. This man was wearing very old clothing, layered to keep him warm, and a pair of old worn out sneakers. The only thing that made him a soldier in any way was the AK47 he gripped with his left hand. Another guard quickly came over and surprisingly introduced himself to me as Massoud. Massoud actually spoke English quite well. He later told me his father was a doctor before all of the wars broke out, and he learned to speak English at a very young age.

Since it was after midnight, it was very quiet on the streets beyond the compound. This gave Massoud and I a chance to talk, and we got to know each other for a few minutes. Massoud then began to explain the dangers of the area. Massoud stressed to me to always be ready no matter how quiet things may seem.

Massoud said, "Any one of these cars, at any moment, can stop right in front of us and explode. If you're paying attention and know what to look for, you will live. If you are not ready, you will die."

Massoud continued to talk to me about ways to identify possible car bombs and pedestrian suicide bombers. He also told me about other threats I would certainly be confronted with in Afghanistan.

Later in the night, Massoud told me more about himself. He said he was 27, which came as a surprise since he looked like he was at least forty-five. Massoud said life had been very hard for him and he has been at war since he was a very young boy. As a child he was a Mujahedeen fighter against the Soviets. After the Soviets pulled out of Afghanistan, Massoud's home area became entangled in civil fighting by rival groups, and he was fighting again. Massoud enjoyed a very short period of peace in his life, until the Taliban began a rise to power in Afghanistan.

Massoud became involved in the fight against the Taliban and was imprisoned and tortured by them for three years. Massoud told stories of his life to pass the night, and many of them were truly heart breaking. I have never felt as sorry for anyone as I felt for Massoud. In America we think of our war veterans as being tough, but this guy is not a war veteran; his entire life is war.

Massoud said to me, "I was Mujahedeen, and I am still Mujahedeen. We have little in this world except for the honor of our word. I will always protect you, as you do the same for me," as he stuck out his hand to me.

I shook Massoud's hand and told him, "It's a deal."

The rest of the night passed without incident, and my first night on duty in Afghanistan is over. It is just before eight o'clock now, and the street is alive with pedestrians, rickety carts, old cars, bicycles, and even donkeys. The people in the streets are all extremely poor looking and dressed in rags. This place is unlike anything I have ever seen.

February 26, 2003:

Today has been pretty quiet. Around one o'clock in the morning, while I was on-duty, I heard two bombs explode off in the distance. I guess they were not really close enough to cause any concern.

Maybe it is just because I am new in country, but it gets scary down here at night. Sitting in a small fighting position, late at night and all alone, gets creepy, especially when bombs go off. The fighting positions, we call them OPs, are basically a small plywood shed with a tin roof, positioned randomly along the compound's perimeter walls, and they are about eight or nine feet above the street below. They are surrounded by sandbags, and the large openings on the front and sides are covered by chicken wire to help protect you from rocks, bottles, or whatever else someone can throw. The dents, dings, bullet holes, and other damage show that they have taken quite a few hits. Each OP is about four feet by four feet and maybe 4 or five feet high. They are each supplied with a plastic chair, an M249 machinegun, one thousand rounds of ammunition, and an AT4 rocket launcher. There is no electricity in the OP, but there really is not a need for it; the last thing you want to do is light yourself up in here. One quick flash of light and a sniper will know exactly where you are.

I am starting to get very homesick, and this place is starting to become very real. I missed so much about home last night. It was so quiet in the OP, all I had time to do was think, wonder, and miss everything. Each and every person has had a bad day at one point or another, but you usually get to go home at the end, relax, and start over. There is no "going home" here; this is home.

Other than the two explosions earlier in the night, it was complete silence. It was just me all alone with my thoughts. You never really appreciate the little things in life until everything has been taken away. It is the details that make us happy, the little things. I would trade anything for the opportunity to enjoy a hot pizza, a cold beer, and a funny movie tonight. I never would have thought something so little could mean so much.

February 27, 2003:

Tonight started off slowly. It was very quiet, no pedestrians or cars, and I guess you could even say it was boring. I heard periodic gunshots throughout the night; some were single shots and some were full automatic bursts. Most of them sounded a distance off, but a few exchanges were a little too close for comfort.

After shift, at eight o'clock in the morning, two team members and I decided to go out of the compound. Whenever you leave the compound, it is always a good idea to bring a local you can trust to help you get around and translate for you. It has to be someone you can absolutely trust, and we brought Massoud. Massoud basically told us that if shit hits the fan, follow him and we will be fine.

We went to an area of Kabul the troops call Chicken Street. It is very densely populated and extremely poor. Approximately one third of the people in this area are homeless and struggling for survival. We drove to Chicken Street in a Land Cruiser, wearing body armor and armed with an array of handguns, machineguns, and assault rifles. The second we pulled into the area, people would try to open the Land Cruiser's doors every time we stopped. Pointing a 9mm at them did not faze them one bit; they still tried relentlessly to open the locked doors.

We found the best area to park, though I did not find it so hot, and we were swarmed by people as we exited the vehicle. They were all peasants hoping to get from us anything we were willing to offer. One woman in a burqa approached us, and she was crying heavily. She made a motion to her mouth with her hand as if she was eating through the burqa, and she then pointed to a small boy. The boy looked to be around eight years old and was laying on the edge of the road against the curb. He was barely clothed, unconscious, and appeared very malnourished. As we got closer to him, he almost looked as though he was not even alive.

As we shoved past the woman, she grabbed a hold of me. Massoud immediately responded by pointing his AK47 at her and shoving the barrel into her chest. Massoud pushed the rifle into her chest so hard she fell backwards to the ground. The woman began to cry even louder and it became more of a wailing sound. Massoud looked at me and told me the boy died two days ago, and to forget about them. Forget about them? How?

We wandered the area and saw so many people selling things from either a makeshift cart or from a rug spread across the sidewalk. People were selling everything from daily necessity items, to food, to bootleg videos, and even knives and guns. There was commotion and noise everywhere, but all I could hear was the sound of that woman crying in my head.

February 28, 2003:

It was a very quiet day today, thank God. It was kind of rainy all day, so I suppose that either forced people inside or kept them busy trying to stay warm and dry.

I have been here for almost a week now, and I am constantly seeing new customs of the Afghan culture. Sometimes they are interesting, sometimes they are strange, and sometimes they are just shocking. Since I arrived in Kabul, I have noticed a lot of men hugging, kissing, and holding hands together. Many of the men wear nail polish, and I have seen some wearing lipstick. Not just one or two, but a lot of them. Me and another American soldier talked to Massoud and asked him about this.

Massoud explained to us that in Afghanistan women and men do not mingle, and dating is not only strictly forbidden it is also a completely unknown practice to many Afghans. Massoud told us that even married men are very rarely seen in public with their wives. Massoud said most marriages are arranged, and a family will essentially sell their daughter to the potential husband that can afford the most. Since men are allowed more than one wife in Afghanistan, you end up with one wealthier man having multiple wives and many men having nothing. Massoud explained that when children are born, females are considered undesirable and very often do not survive to adulthood. This creates a lot of men who will never date a girl, or even meet a girl outside of their own family. As a result, in some instances, these men "date" each other.

Massoud said although homosexuality is forbidden in Islam and in Afghanistan, it is much easier to hide than being seen in public with a woman. The very idea of male/female mingling is not only considered taboo in culture, it is forbidden by law. The penalty for premarital sex or dating can be as high as death. The typical method of execution for such an offense is called stoning. Massoud explained that the man and woman are placed standing in a hole and buried to their waist. Family members and villagers then begin throwing a stockpile of stones at the couple until they are dead. Massoud pointed towards the road and indicated that the field near the compound was used for such executions. He said, "Stay here long enough and you'll see one."

After hearing Massoud's explanation, I began to understand why so many men show such affection towards one another. I do not think they are necessarily homosexual in our sense of the word. I think the men just utilize the only option they have for affection: one another.

Massoud also said child abuse is extremely common in Kabul. He said many children are raped every day and there is no one championing for their rights or safety. With so many homeless children in Kabul, and virtually no protection for them, it is out of control. Massoud said by the time many boys reach adulthood they have likely been raped multiple times throughout their childhood, causing many to become numb to the idea of having sex with another male.

It is absolutely shocking and heartbreaking to see how women and children are treated here. I have never imagined anything like this.

March 1, 2003:

It was very quiet throughout the night, but things got very busy right after dawn. Yesterday, a British soldier was out in Kabul when an Afghan approached and shot him. The Brit's body armor stopped the bullet, and he returned fire, killing the Afghan. A lot of locals are now angry over the shooting of an Afghan, and many decided to protest.

A protest consisting of about five or six hundred people, in an area just outside of the compound, quickly turned into a riot. Things got worse until a hand grenade was thrown from the crowd into the Afghan Police compound across the street from us. Two Afghan Police Officers were seriously injured, and the Afghan force responded by opening fire on the crowd. Three officers posted on the roof of the Police Station began shooting into the crowd with their AK47s, causing people to run and clearing the crowd. After several short bursts of fire, some people were trampling one another to flee, and others were carrying away those wounded by the gunfire. Within fifteen minutes, the riot was over and everyone was gone. I cannot even imagine how many people may have just been killed.

The Afghan Police are very brutal and corrupt. The Police Chief is actually a former warlord who once controlled a large area of territory during the Taliban regime. It is said that he uses his police to traffic weapons and drugs, eliminate competition, and strong arm anyone out of any money he can. I have even heard rumors that he is paid by the Americans to remain "loyal" to us. How true that is, I have no idea.

The police here also seem free to rob at will. They set up security checkpoints, but they are more like toll booths. They allow American forces to pass through unbothered, but they rob Afghans of whatever they can find. Most of these people do not have anything to begin with, and then they are robbed by the so-called police. It just makes no sense to me.

Today was a very nerve-racking day, but it is over now. I am starting to get into a groove here, and I am trying to make it feel like a home. I try each day to go to the gym on the compound. It is not the best, but all things considered it is really not bad. I eat breakfast, and then I will either leave the compound for a mission or try to sleep. After a few hours of sleep, I wake up and do it all over again. It is becoming really repetitive, but I am hoping the routine makes the time fly.

March 2, 2003:

It was a very quiet night again; long, dark, and cold. The lonely quiet gave me a chance to talk with Massoud and learn more about him and his people. Massoud said he was a mujahedeen fighter from an area called the Panjshir Valley.

Massoud said the word mujahedeen means "holy warrior," but the true mujahedeen think of themselves as freedom fighters. When the Russians invaded Afghanistan in the 1970s, they planned to make Afghanistan free of religion and ban Islam. The people resisted and the mujahedeen fought a long, bloody war against the Russians. After many years of fighting, the mujahedeen triumphed and the Russians left Afghanistan.

Shortly after the Russians left, the Taliban rose to power. Massoud described the Taliban as a group of men who hid behind the religion of Islam and used Islamic law to control society, although their true motive was not religious. Massoud claims the true reason for having complete control of the people was so they could also have complete control of the money, guns, drugs, and territory in Afghanistan. The mujahedeen rose again and fought the Taliban, with many being either killed or captured and subsequently tortured. This time the mujahedeen fighters had far less success than against the Russians.

Massoud then described to me a new breed of radical Muslim fighters who are declaring a jihad, or holy war, and are also calling themselves mujahedeen fighters. Massoud said these men are not freedom fighters; they are killing innocent people with car bombs, rockets, landmines, and drive-by shootings. These men torture, maim, and ruin lives; they destroy the lives around them, rather than protect. According to Massoud, these new mujahedeen fighters are not, and never will be, true mujahedeen warriors.

He also explained terrorism in Afghanistan. Massoud said the terrorist leaders try to justify their actions by calling it the poorest nation in the world striking out against the wealthiest. The fact is however, the terrorist leaders are actually very wealthy. Massoud said they are really trying to serve their own selfish motives and use the most impressionable people they can manage to manipulate. Massoud sadly said there are many people in Afghanistan who have never had an education, and they quickly follow the false teachings of these self-proclaimed leaders. Most Afghans do see through the lies, but many do not. As a result, violence has become a way of life in this country.

Other than talking with Massoud, not a thing went on last night.

March 3, 2003:

The night shift was very slow, it seems like a pattern is developing. Sometimes I actually enjoy the silence of sitting all alone in the OP at night; all you can do is think. I think a lot about myself and my life. I think about who I really am, where I am going in life, and what I am actually accomplishing right now. I have never really stopped to do that, and it is actually very nice to like the answers that you find. I think a lot of people should do this more often. If you like what you find, it is wonderful. If you do not like what you find, it is never too late to start making changes.

I have been wondering a lot about what will happen when I go home. I wonder where I will live, what I will be doing, and other things like that. We got our first chance to call home last night. I called my wife, but there was no answer. Hopefully she will be there next time.

As the morning rolled around, I did not get to go to bed; instead, we went out on a mission. Last night, a British civilian was shot and killed, and as a result we are going to be putting a lot of military presence in the area of the shooting. A total of ten of us loaded up into two Suburbans, and rolled out of the compound and into the Kabul madness. I call it that because the traffic here is absolutely insane. Just like every other aspect of life here, there are essentially no rules. People drive on whatever side of the road they choose, and they drive as fast or slow as they want. There are no stop signs or traffic lights, and the right of way basically goes to whoever has the biggest balls. To top it all off, the streets are filled with a medley of every mode of transportation imaginable, with no one giving a shit about the others. The bicyclists are the worst as they are everywhere. On our way out of the compound, we hit one guy with our mirror so hard it knocked him off his bike. I felt bad, but we cannot stop for anything.

We got to the area of Kabul we were patrolling, and it was relatively calm. There were a lot of people around, but nothing seemed like trouble, and everyone was just going about their daily business. When we parked and got out of the Suburbans, no one approached us, and there were no beggars. It was strange; people would not even make eye contact. As the day went on, we learned that the rumor on the street was that an American was killed and not a British civilian. The locals were scared that we were there for revenge. I think they viewed us as being angry and armed, and no one wanted to give us an excuse to fire.

We were in a part of Kabul that is very badly ruined and extremely impoverished. Most of the buildings had heavy signs of war with walls blown apart, bullet holes, and collapsed roofs. Even the road and sidewalk had craters from past explosions. The main street, if you want to call it that, had numerous narrow alleyways branching off of it. The alleys were littered with garbage, and each alley had families living out of makeshift shelters. Many of the "homes" within the alleys were just old boxes covered with plastic. The most shocking thing was to see how many children seem to be living in these alleys all alone.

The children were all very dirty, and their clothes were absolutely disgusting. The amazing part though, these kids were still kids. I saw a lot of them playing with what they could, and they actually seemed to be enjoying themselves. I saw one group of kids laughing and giggling while they were playing with an old, deflated soccer ball. When no adults are looking the children will sometimes give us a smile and a "thumbs up." No matter how much life sucks for them, kids are kids.

To see a kid living a life like that and still able to smile, it sparks an emotion inside of you that is impossible to describe with words. Part of me wishes more than anything that these kids could have a better life, but I know the reality is a quarter of them will not even be alive in five years; yet, they smile.

March 4, 2003:

After the midnight to eight shift in the OP, a group of us loaded up and went back out to patrol again. Driving through Kabul is one thing, but when you stop and get out of the vehicle, you are in a whole other world. Twelve of us went out, and we walked in three-man teams. It is a voluntary mission for me today as it was another squad's assignment. Walking around, patrolling this area is such a rush; I cannot get enough of it. After yesterday's patrol, I laid in my bed in total darkness for a few hours before OP duty. I could still feel the adrenaline that had built up in my body, and its rush was amazing.

During today's patrol, there were a lot more people out on the streets, and there were a lot more guns. I know that if shit goes down, my body armor will stop one or two rounds from an AK47, but after that I would be in some serious shit. I tried not to let that thought run through my mind, but when you see so many rifles out in the streets, it's hard to ignore them. You see men who look as old as sixty, and boys as young as twelve, carrying a rifle. It is freaky.

All of the little kids really seem interested in us. When we walk past them, they smile and wave or give a "thumbs up." The older kids on the other hand, teenagers seem to hate us. They will tell us to go home, give us the finger, or spit towards us. They do not speak English, but a very common phrase we keep hearing is "America no good. America go home." It does stand to reason; they are teenagers and need to rebel against something: us.

The streets were very tense today. During the patrol we had to check a lot of people, a lot of vehicles, and a lot of storefronts for anything suspicious or dangerous. Our current orders are not to take weapons from civilians as long as they are only in possession of a single rifle. We were told that order will be changing soon, but for now it is what it is.

Stopping and searching civilians is not very stressful, but searching cars get very nerve-racking. Car bombs are the weapon of choice for the Taliban in Kabul. When a car is left unattended for too long, or a driver is acting strange, it becomes our job to make sure it is safe. Checking vehicles can only be described as absolutely, fucking terrifying. With each second that passes by, your ass puckers tighter, and you pray the thing does not explode on you. The only thing that keeps me going is to constantly tell myself that if it does explode it will be quick, and I will not feel a thing. The adrenaline really is one hell of a rush, though!

Another amazing thing is how hard the Afghans work. I watched a group of men working to remove the rubble from a blown out building. They were not using heavy equipment and machinery; instead, they were using spade shovels and a wheelbarrow. All of the work here is done by hand or, if they are lucky, with the help of a horse or donkey. Most of the people here cannot afford a donkey, so it is very common to see a man pulling a cart filled with rock and debris rather than an animal doing the job.

Most of the workers are very beaten and worn by a brutal existence. They are all very dirty, most with long and mangy beards. Many of the men are even working without shoes. I could not help but wonder: if that was me, and I was being forced to work that hard, how would I look at life? My view would probably be a lot different than what I see today. I feel absolutely terrible for these people, and even after the adrenaline fades, that sadness only grows stronger. I have seen things that have made me sad and people that I've felt sorrow for, but never anything like this. We have all read about poverty and starvation around the world, but I never imagined I would be witnessing it firsthand. On one hand I wish I did not have to see this, but on the other I hope it causes me to never again take anything for granted. I hope this makes me appreciate every last thing I have been blessed with in life.

March 5, 2003:

Today was a good day. The midnight shift in the OP flew by and before I knew it, it was dawn. Right after shift, I put my name in to use the compound's computer to email home. When it was my turn, I trembled with excitement as I waited for my inbox to load. It was almost like Christmas morning. Who would ever think that something as simple as an email could make you feel so incredible.

I got an email from my wife, but I feel almost confused, for lack of a better term. Every email I receive from her just seems to be a reply to something I had previously sent, or she is writing for a specific reason: a forgotten password, a combination, or she needs to know how to do something around the house. She never sends sweet emails or special notes. I know the other guys have girls back home who send sexy emails with "interesting" pictures, sweet e-cards, and things like that. I check my email whenever I can, hoping to get something like that, and I never do. One of the guys got a care package from home filled with candy and magazines, and his girlfriend threw in one of her shirts so he could smell her. The second care package she sent had a pair of lace sexy underwear. It makes me wonder why I am not getting anything like that. With nothing but time on my hands, it makes me wonder about everything. This really sucks. I cannot help but worry that I did something wrong.

After using the computer, I hit the gym for a little bit. The gym is my favorite way to unwind and blow off the steam and excess adrenaline from the day. I made a promise to myself that I will go every day and get everything out.

Once I was back in the room, I managed my way through the little space there was to get to my bed. Our room is now filled with bunks and gear, and it smells like a brutal combination of feet and ass. Our plumbing shit the bed almost a week ago, so none of us have showered in days. The smell in this room is absolutely horrendous, and I actually signed up for this.

March 6, 2003:

During shift last night, I was in the OP when there were three small explosions around four o'clock in the morning. About ten minutes later a fourth, much larger explosion rang out. The first three were far enough from the compound that they did not cause much alarm. The fourth one was much closer, and it was strong enough to rattle my OP. I am still not sure what was bombed; we usually don't find out until later the next day and sometimes the day after.

After shift ended, we went on another mission. Today we went to a remote village about ninety-five miles west of Kabul. We received our briefing, and from the get-go it was very unsettling. The village was about four hours from Kabul, so it was going to be a long ride. The route through the rural area is not often used, and the area is notorious for landmines. Lastly, our destination is very pro-Taliban and anti-American. What could possibly go wrong?

The powers that be determined we would travel in civilian SUVs rather than military HUMVEEs. Five of us loaded up in a single Land Cruiser and moved out. Most of the trip was uneventful, and the road was old, narrow and at times almost non-existent. The landscape looked a lot like the area outside of Las Vegas, nothing but desert and mountains. Four hours into the drive, we passed through a small village. The road winding through the village was very tight, forcing us to pass through very slow.

Each person we passed leered into the truck and looked at us like we were from Mars. They knew we were Americans, and it was very obvious we were not welcomed. A lot of the men wore a green strip of cloth tied around their upper arm, indicating they were Taliban.

I was very, very far outside of my comfort level. After a few minutes we had cleared the village without any incidents, but in Afghanistan the situation can always change in a split second.

About ten minutes outside of the village, we entered a blind curve along a cliff. As we exited the curve, there was an old Soviet T-55 tank blocking the road. We were stopped about thirty yards from the tank, and an Afghan was manning the tank's 20mm machinegun which was pointed right at us. Even though that tank was an old Russian piece of shit, that machinegun would rip our vehicle to shreds. We were very quickly approached by three Afghans with AK47 rifles. The Afghans spoke no English, and the situation became extremely tense. One of the Afghans was shouting something at us, and he was obviously very pissed off at us. The Sergeant in the front seat ordered everyone to stay still and not do a thing. We were in no position to make a move because of that machinegun.

None of us spoke, and we were all scared shitless. I did not know, and I guess I still do not, if this was just a random checkpoint set up to rob people or if the village had notified them we were coming and we were about to be taken. An American head is worth a lot of money in Afghanistan. After a very long and tense twenty or so minute wait, an Afghan arrived who spoke broken English.

The English-speaking Afghan demanded to know who was in charge, and the Sergeant identified himself. The Afghan started yelling something about us having hostile intentions and accused us of trespassing on their land. After a minute of arguing, the Sergeant told the Afghan that we called in on our radio and reported the tank and our location. He told the Afghan that if we do not call in again in the next five minutes, Bagram is going to send out the A-10 war planes to kill them, level their village, and destroy their tank. The Sergeant argued with the Afghan again, and after a few minutes the Afghan walked towards the tank while waving his hand in a circular motion in the air. I heard the tank's diesel engine fire up, and the tank pulled off from the roadway.

The sergeant told the driver to go slow, but start driving. As the SUV slowly moved forward, I was cringing and half expecting the machine gun to start firing. It never did, and we made it out fine. Like I said, I do not know if they were just a checkpoint to rob people or if we were almost taken, but I cannot get a thought out of my mind: what would have happened if they had taken us? We did not have nearly enough ammo to fight our way out of there, and no one even knew where we were. I just imagine myself wearing some jumpsuit and having my head cut off, for the world to see on Al-Jazeera.

We finished out the mission and then drove back to Kabul. When we passed through the same area where we had previously encountered the tank, it was gone and the village was practically deserted. They probably figured an airstrike was coming and hauled ass. We got back to Camp Eagle safely, and now I am here writing about the day while I get ready to take a nap before reporting for OP duty.

March 7, 2003:

After shift today, we went to the local bazaar. It is an open area where the Afghans lay out blankets and display all sorts of items for sale. It is the Afghan equivalent of a flea market. It was a fun way to spend the day as merchants were selling antique guns, knives, videos, jewelry, handmade rugs, and more. As you pass each merchant, they greet you with, "Hello, my friend. Items very nice." I think they all learned their limited English from the same person.

The fun part of the bazaar is the bargaining. Central Asia is believed by many to be the birthplace of trade and commerce, and the Afghans love to haggle. I found a marble and hand carved wood chess set that would easily sell for three to four hundred dollars in America. I asked how much, and the merchant punched "40" into his calculator. I responded with "15," and he shook his head while typing in "25." I typed in "20," and the merchant shook his head and retyped "25." I turned to walk away and within five steps I heard him shout, "My friend!" I returned, and the merchant humbly accepted the twenty dollar offer.

The day was filled with similar encounters. There may have been a few deals at the bazaar, but most of the stuff was just trash. It was just fun to be outside and interacting with people in a positive manner. Yeah, it was a good day.

March 8, 2003:

During the midnight shift, a German ISAF team was traveling down a main road near Camp Eagle when they were ambushed. A bomb was placed along the road, and as the ISAF vehicle was passing by, the bomb was detonated. Two German soldiers were killed and three seriously injured.

After OP shift, my squad was assigned to provide security for a Colonel who was going to a meeting in a notoriously dangerous area of Kabul. We went to a new school for children ages five through twelve. The school is scheduled to open soon, and an American military civil affairs unit is making final preparations with desks, paper, pencils, and other supplies.

The ride to the school was a little unsettling as we drove by the scene of last night's bombing. You never know when you are next.

As we approached the school, I was in an area that words alone could never describe. It was a neighborhood jam packed with apartment buildings so close that a car could not be driven between them. This place can only be described as pure slum. Each building was between five and ten stories and shaped like a shoebox. Very few of the windows still had glass in them, and a makeshift clothesline hung from every window. Each and every building was so dilapidated that it seemed impossible they were still used as housing; however, the clothes hanging from each window told otherwise.

People were everywhere, fighting to swarm our vehicles, and many tried to open the doors as we crept by them. I was shocked to see how many people were very obviously high on something. Massoud, who came as our translator, told us this neighborhood is infested with opium and heroin. Robbery, murder, and squalor are all a part of daily life for everyone living in this area. Massoud said the children are particularly vulnerable in this area because of this crime. As with every other part of Kabul, there were lots of children. The difference here being that these kids were not playing and making the best of anything; their lives are beyond horrible. Looking at this was gut wrenching.

When we parked, there was a row of several shops on our left side. These are not the typical shops you would think of in an American plaza; instead, they are just a row of barely covered shacks offering some service or another. One guy was fixing bicycle tires while another was doing metal work. One of the shops is blown to shit, and the burned out car that carried the bomb is still in front of the shop. Violence is everywhere in this place.

I think that is all that I really want to write about today. I could go on for hours about that shithole, but I am getting very tired. Since I am still writing, it goes without saying that the day ended safely. All ten fingers and toes are still wiggling.

Earlier this morning, as we drove through the scene of last night's bombing, and then later when I was looking at the remains of the other car bomb, I could not help but wonder how many times you can tempt fate and still walk away. How many times can you keep pulling straws before you finally pull the short one? I wonder if I am really going to get through this.

March 9, 2003:

Lately we have been noticing a lot of suspicious people, all just hanging around in the streets surrounding the compound. Just the other day, dayshift soldiers in the OPs reported seeing Afghans in the street taking notes as they walked the perimeter just beyond our walls.

Tonight, at the start of my shift and just a few minutes after midnight, a minivan drove around the streets of the compound a few times. I got out of the OP and laid flat on the top of the wall, using sandbags as cover. As the radio lit up with chatter, I could hear the Sergeant on duty telling us all to be ready to hit the van. I saw the van turning from the south end of the compound and traveling north on the street along the west wall. I had my M249 aimed dead on the driver's side, just waiting to kill every fucking thing in that van. As I watched the van coming towards me, I heard the sergeant yelling, "Get someone with an AT-4 on that west wall." An AT-4 rocket launcher will take the whole van out, but not before me and my machinegun could do the same fucking thing. I could hear the engine of the van revving as it sped along the street towards me. I rested my finger on the trigger and began to gently squeeze, waiting for the order to take out the driver. The Sergeant then ordered us to stand down. As the van passed the south gate, the guards saw the passenger holding a video camera, and the

Sergeant wanted to have patrol units outside the gate go after the vehicle rather than us engage.

I can still hear the engine screaming as that van was speeding towards my location on the wall, and I still feel the anxiety of wondering if I was going to kill the driver or, even worse, if the god damned thing was going to blow up near me.

We have recently been getting a lot of information suggesting local Taliban and Al Qaeda fighters are planning an assault on the compound. The plan we have been hearing is they intend to simultaneously detonate multiple car bombs along the exterior walls and the main gates, and then use the chaos to have fighters armed with small arms rush in, killing as many as they can. We thought it was all bullshit, but tonight really tells me there is something to it. It might actually happen. The passenger with the camera was videotaping our reaction to the van. They will most likely analyze the video and identify the most vulnerable points. This shit is real.

Afghanistan has been hit very hard by a drought for the past several years, but the rain has returned this year. The growing season is right around the corner and, with the recent rain, the season should be very productive. We are all hoping that people will be more concerned with growing crops and ending the famine than with fighting and attacking coalition troops.

Another hope for peace in Afghanistan is the recent surge in the economy. The locals here live in a poverty that is beyond comprehension for most other people, but it is showing signs of improvement. With troops from around the world in Afghanistan, money is flowing in, and it is starting to trickle down to some people. There are public works jobs starting to appear, some people are working directly for the American military, and others are starting small businesses. Granted these small businesses might be along the lines of repairing bicycle tires, but at least it is some type of work. The problem is far from fixed, but I think some people here may see a glimmer of hope, a hope they have not seen for a long, long time.

I just hope the rain, along with a new sense of hope for many Afghans, is enough to curb the violence that is ripping this place apart.

March 10, 2003:

Massoud and I were talking at the main gate last night and just killing time. Massoud has been trying to teach me Dari, the language people speak in Kabul, but I am not really very interested. When I leave here, when will I ever need to speak Dari? Pretty useless, but he has taught me a few useful things: "Show me your hands," "Get down on the ground," and "Don't move or you will be shot."

Massoud was also telling me about Islam and Islamic prayers. He really seems intent on us being as safe as possible, and he wants us to constantly look for specific things when we are on patrol in the city. One of the things he wants us to watch for is prayer. Massoud said Afghan Muslims have a very specific set of rules to follow just before and just after someone's death. Massoud said suicide bombers very often follow some of these rules, and these can cause them to stand out in a crowd. Massoud taught me a few key prayer phrases to listen for. If we see someone sitting in a car or walking in the street praying, we want to be somewhere else and fast!

The night was very quiet, and there was virtually no activity on the streets. Everyone thinks that being in a war is nothing but non-stop action and fighting. I thought that too before I came here. It is actually ninety percent boredom mixed with ten percent shitting your pants, and there is absolutely nothing in between. You are either bored crazy or knee deep in some shitty mess.

We have been trying to change that and find little ways to have fun. We managed to find a TV and some bootleg DVDs for sale on Chicken Street, and one of the guys had someone from home send a DVD player. When we do have down time, we have been watching movies lately, and it is actually a lot of fun. We'll grab a bunch of snacks from the care packages we received, throw on a movie, and crowd around the TV. It's funny how something like watching a movie can be so much fun when you stop taking it for granted.

A few of the other guys are also into Jiu Jitsu, so a few of us chipped in and bought a couple of sets of heavy gloves to start our own version of a training center. That is actually some of the most fun I have had here in Afghanistan; however, we do not get to do that very often because we need to keep it very quiet. If the command staff ever found out we were beating the shit out of each other for fun, they would put a stop to that very quickly, and I think that is half the fun of it.

Another activity we have found to pass the time is gambling, and we gamble on everything. We bet on coin tossing, on cards, and on anything else which we cannot control the outcome. Some of the guys have started a new gambling pastime that is very popular with everyone. We will all start looking under rocks and old boards until we find one scorpion and one camel spider. Camel spiders are very large, hairy spiders that are creepy as can be. Once they have one of each, they will put them in a box. The two will fight, and everyone bets which one will win.

I have the worst luck in the world when it comes to gambling, so I just hang on to my money. The only time I gamble is when I eat the food from outside of our compound. The food usually goes down and comes out just fine, but other times not so much. Sometimes the food here gives you diarrhea so bad you need an I.V. to replace all the fluids you have lost. Everyone calls it the "Hajji blowout."

Supplies come and go; sometimes supplies are good, and sometimes they're slim. When supplies are slim we still get food on the compound, but when we're out on missions we need to do what we can to eat. When that situation arises, we are usually left to survive off of the local economy. We will buy meat or live animals from desert nomads, and it is usually not *that* bad. I use the phrase "not that bad" quite loosely. Sometimes it gets rough, and you end up with a case of that Hajji blowout.

March 11, 2003:

Today was only day eighteen in Afghanistan. In some ways the time seems to be flying by, but in others it is going so slowly. Before we got to Afghanistan, my unit was in upstate New York for over a month of training. I have been away for about two months now, and I am really missing home. I hoped that as time went on I would get used to it, but I really have not. I know I still have a long road ahead of me, and I probably should not even think of being home. It is easier said than done, and my mind drifts back there a lot.

It seems like every day is the same thing, over and over again. Nothing pleasant ever happens here, and no news is ever good news. Every day there is some new threat against us, or there something else to be worried about. Every time we leave the relative safety of the compound I see something else that makes me sick, and I possibly come one step closer to my card being pulled.

I have this weird feeling of emptiness inside. It seems as though everything good in my life has been replaced with something bad. Everything that I used to look forward to has been replaced with something I either fear or loathe. Everyone I loved has been replaced with feelings of sadness, and they need to be bottled up and never shown. I have a job to do here, and I am going to do it. I can deal with these feelings some other day, but for now they just need to stay locked away.

Sometimes I wonder if I am the only one who feels this way, but I know I see it in some of the other guys as well. We will come back from a mission and guys will say things like, "I just want to leave this place alive." Never did I imagine it would be like this.

I think I had it in my mind that we would be in the middle of nowhere, twiddling our thumbs all day. The reality though, is we are a combat unit, attached to the Third Special Forces Group, in the most dangerous place in the world, and it scares the living shit out of me. Sometimes I am very afraid. I never show it, and I always do my job, but sometimes I think the fear slowly chips away at me. Every time we leave the compound, either something happens or we see something that just makes my heart stop and forces me to pray it is not about to happen. Then I breathe a sigh of relief when it turns out to be ok, and I wait for the next thing to happen. It is never ending, but every night I do my duty on the wall, and almost every day I go out on patrol in the city.

The patrols are not physically demanding; in that aspect, they are easy. We patrol on foot, in three or four man teams, just walking around the streets and looking for anyone or anything suspicious. I am a machine gunner and I always carry my M249. I just wish I was able to carry more ammunition than I can fit in my rucksack. I worry that if we get locked down in a fire fight, I will run out of ammo far too quickly. I sent an email to my wife asking her to send me a plain black backpack that I can wear in reverse on my chest, to carry a few more drums of ammo, but I still have not received it yet. Every email she sends says, "No haven't sent it yet, but I will tomorrow." It was tomorrow five days ago, and I need that thing now.

I also asked her to send me a new holster for my 9mm, because the issued holster basically sucks. She emailed back saying she cannot find one, so I am guessing that means I am not getting it. From the sound of things, I probably will not be getting the backpack either. Sometimes I am not sure what to say besides, "Whatever."

March 12, 2003:

Tonight seems as though people are getting ready for something. All night long, cars have been driving past the compound, with people yelling from them and honking their horns. A convoy of vehicles circled the compound four or five times. The vehicles were old pickup trucks with people crammed into the back of each truck. Someone in the lead truck was waving a Taliban era flag.

A little later, less than thirty minutes after the trucks circled the compound, I heard three rapid explosions within a half mile of the compound. Within minutes of the explosions, I heard an exchange of gunfire. The volley of gunshots lasted for about thirty to forty-five seconds before they stopped. Our radio lit up with reports that another unit's security patrol was taking sniper fire from an unknown number of hostiles. Within minutes the situation was over, and the other unit was reporting one American casualty. Then it was dead calm for the rest of the night.

An Afghan guard, Khalid, speaks broken English, and I asked him why some Afghan people are so hostile towards the Americans, when we are only here to help this country.

He said the causes of Afghanistan's problems are very complicated. He said the vast majority of Afghans want the stability that America is trying to bring. He explained how the Afghans, young and old, fought to the death to drive the Soviets out of Afghanistan, and would have fought until every last Afghan was dead. He then said, "If we didn't want the Americans here, we would fight just the same. We don't fight. Most of us don't fight, anyway." He told me that if the Afghans did not want us here, we would be constantly engaged in battle.

The Afghans want freedom just as much as we enjoy ours. However, Afghanistan is not made up of one single group of people but several different tribes. Every tribe has different ethnic, religious, and cultural beliefs, and they rarely see eye-to-eye. Each tribe wants the entire nation of Afghanistan to be molded around their own ideals, and because of this they fight constantly.

The warlords take advantage of these rivalries by stimulating fighting between these groups for their own benefit. The fighters are essentially the warlord's personal army, and they become pawns in a greater game of chess. If one particular tribe or warlord benefits from the people fighting with the Americans, they shift their anger towards us and get everyone riled up. To stop this, a lot of these warlords have been offered positions in Afghanistan's new, emerging government as well as top police and military positions. This game creates a power struggle for everyone trying to come out the victor, with as many spoils as possible.

When you take all of this and add in religious extremism, you have a breeding ground for terrorist activity. Groups like the Taliban, Al Qaeda, and the Holy Islamic Jihad have used this power struggle along with misinformation to turn people against America and the new Afghan government. They have turned this country into a powder keg that is set to explode.

These fighters hide and blend in among Afghanistan's population of thirty-four million people. They come out to fight very quickly, and then melt right back into the population. They wear no uniforms, have no insignia, and they are very hard to find. The area between Kabul and the Pakistani border is filled with these fighters. Fighting one second and gone the next. Their weapons of choice are improvised roadside bombs, car bombs, explosive mortars, and rocket attacks.

These people who are against the ideas of the western nations are now seeing a light of hope for many people in Afghanistan. New schools and hospitals are opening all the time, and there is slowly a new way of thinking in Afghanistan. They want to crush that hope and attack any target they can.

This place is very complicated and has many issues, with extreme violence often being the result of those issues. It is to the point that violence is the only way of life many Afghans now know. Like Sean said when I first got here, this place is fucked up.

March 13, 2003:

The midnight shift was slow tonight. We had rain almost all night, and I am assuming it kept everyone inside. Around six o'clock in the morning, a convoy of SUVs came rushing to the compound. A very popular national news figure, (name has been removed), came to the compound to include some of our operations in a story he is doing.

We had no idea he was coming, and after shift he spent time talking to a few of us. I went to the dining room to have breakfast where I got to eat with him, and he actually turned out to be a very nice guy. He was eager to meet with everyone, and he was happy to shake hands and take pictures. It definitely added an interesting and positive twist to the day.

They put together a team to provide additional security for his trip to an area called Gardez. This is a notoriously dangerous area, and the ride out there is known to be very risky. There are a lot of Taliban supporters in that area and reports of active Al Qaeda camps. I decided not to volunteer for this one and got to take the day off.

I went to the gym, and then got cleaned up. I caught up on writing some letters home, and then I cleaned my weapons and sorted my gear. Now I am here writing and thinking about going to bed early. If I go to bed now, I will get a good seven hours of sleep before I need to get back up for the midnight shift. This will be the first time I have gotten more than four hours of sleep in almost two weeks. I guess that means, "Good night."

March 14, 2003:

It was raining again, so it made for another long, lonely night keeping watch in the OP. Around seven o'clock this morning, a bicyclist got hit by a car, along the west wall of the compound, right in front of my position. The bicyclist did not appear to be hurt too bad, and he ended up provoking a yelling match with the driver of the vehicle. Before long, it erupted into an all out brawl between the two of them. Within minutes, there were eight or nine other guys joining in the fight. They were all just random people on the street, and they started joining the fight.

A group of us exited our OPs and gathered along the wall. Half of the goal was to get into a ready position in case this fight was a distraction for something bigger about to happen, and the other half was to just watch the fight. Very quickly, the powers that be decided the brawl was too close to the compound and presented too much of a security risk, and we were ordered to disperse the crowd immediately. We threw two canisters of CS gas into the crowd and as soon as the gas hit the crowd, they scattered.

After shift, my squad was assigned a mission that took us towards the Pakistani border. The Pakistani government is supposed to be an ally of the United States, but the people of Pakistan see things much differently.

The road leading out to our destination is very dangerous and goes right through some very hostile areas. Several convoys have taken enemy fire recently on this route, by snipers supposedly trained in Pakistan.

After about two and a half hours out of Kabul, the ride was very boring until the road began to follow the path of an old dried-out riverbed. The road curved through a pass with ten to fifteen foot rock ledges on either side of us. Our convoy consisted of six HUMVEEs, and I was the gunner for the third vehicle. I knew that entering the pass was dangerous as shit, but we had no way around it.

Half way through the half-mile-long pass, the lead vehicle stopped and I heard a burst of shots ring out. The lead vehicle was mounted with a fifty caliber machine gun, and the sound thundered through the pass as the gunner returned fire. They were around a slight bend, and we could not see exactly what was going on. My field of fire was to the left side, and I kept my mounted M249 fixed upwards at the top of the rock ledge.

As the fifty caliber stopped firing, I could hear the squad leader on the radio yelling, "Move, move, move! Don't bottle up in here. Get the fuck out!" The trucks started moving through pass, as fast as we could. As we pulled through the curve, I could see two men, with cloths covering their faces, about one hundred feet to the left of the convoy. Every gunner in the convoy began firing, and the two snipers pulled back to behind an old wall. It was obvious that we had not hit them. The Sergeant made the call not to chase them down because they could be luring us into a greater trap, and we had a mission that needed to be finished.

I still cannot believe that a bomb was not placed for us in the pass. Al Qaeda and Taliban fighters love using improvised explosives during their attacks. They make their bombs out of old rockets, mortar shells, or landmines.

The whole thing happened so fast, it was over before I knew it. As we pulled out of the pass, it took me a minute to really believe what had just happened. Every vehicle checked in over the radio, announcing no injuries and no damage, so we pressed forward and continued on with the mission. It was kind of surprising how the incident was not very frightening at all, while it was occurring. Once everything was over and done, on the other hand, it was scary to look back on. At the time instinct just took over and my reactions just seemed to happen naturally. I am not sure how to explain it. The rest of the mission went well, and we got to the forward firing base just fine.

The unit I am in is made up of about one hundred and fifty troops, and we are all scattered around different bases in Kabul and Bagram, with about thirty five of us at Camp Eagle. I found out today that one of our guys at another compound, the Kabul Military Training Center, contracted Malaria over there. Afghanistan has a lot of diseases that we do not have in America anymore, such as things like Malaria, Leprosy, and other weird or bizarre illnesses. There is one thing that is absolutely certain about Afghanistan: in one way or another, there is always something here that can hurt you.

March 15, 2003:

Midnight shift was very long and quiet, yet again. Around eight o'clock last night, before I started my OP watch, I was taking a little nap after we got back from a mission. We were woken up and instructed to report to our posts early and double up at every point. I did not know what had happened yet, but I knew there must have been something. I was walking to my assigned OP along the south wall, where I was assigned for the night, and I heard there was just a series of bombings in the area.

As the night went on, I heard more and more and eventually found out there were three bombings, all within two and a half miles of the compound. The closest attack was just a quarter of a mile away. Two were suicide bombings at local shops, and a third was an improvised explosive left along the roadway. No word on casualties yet, and I have no idea if any Americans were targeted. It usually takes a few days for us to get full and accurate information, so I will not know for a little bit.

On the plus side of things, the weather has been getting very nice lately. When I first got here, it was chilly during the day but downright cold at night. The nights are still chilly, but the daytime temperatures seem to be climbing a little more every day. I was expecting it to be hot here all the time, but our elevation in the mountains definitely keeps things chilly during the winter months. It has actually snowed several times since I arrived. When our missions take us further into the mountains, it can get very cold, but it is becoming nice here. The weather is becoming nice anyway.

The squad opened a large care package yesterday, which had been sent by an anonymous sender. It had a volleyball set and some other cool stuff. Our Lieutenant gave us the go ahead to set up the volleyball net in a dirt area adjacent to where we park the trucks. Volleyball should be a fun way to pass the small amount of free time we do have. Other than what I have already written, there is not much else to write about. I am tired, and I am going to bed. Another day is done in Afghanistan.

March 16, 2003:

Last night, I finally had a night off. As midnight was approaching and the rest of my squad was gearing up to head out to their assigned OP, I was gathering movies and snacks from my foot locker and getting ready for my first night to relax in a long time.

Around five-thirty in the morning, I went to use the telephone and check my email. I was able to call my wife for the first time in weeks, and also write to some friends. Good thing I got to do that last night, because all email and telephones were locked down today. American forces are getting ready to invade Iraq and the military is raising the threat level at all military bases and compounds in the Middle East and Central Asia. Part of that increase is to cut off all lines of communication between us and the outside world. It does not really have that big of an impact on me, though. My squad almost never has time for the computer or phones, and when we do, the wait in line is so long it is not even worth it. When we have four or five hours to sleep before we have to be back up for midnight, it is not worth waiting in line for two of those hours just to make a five minute phone call. It is a hard choice to make sometimes, but exhaustion usually wins.

It is very difficult being so cut off from the world and not knowing what is going on. The only information we get is newspaper clippings that are usually weeks old by the time they arrive. Day by day, we have no idea what is going on back home, how our families are doing, or what is happening in our old lives. It is a very cold feeling to be so separated from everything you love.

My night off, though uneventful, was very nice. Watching movies and eating snacks was a way to pretend I was somewhere else for a little while. I could pretend I was somewhere comfortable, somewhere safe, and anywhere but here.

I constantly think about the people who are stuck living in this shit. In five months, I get to leave here and go home. The people who live here have no such hope and little hope for a better way of living any time soon. Every day, when I am on a mission or out on patrol, I look at all of the people who have to endure the kind of life they are given here. I cannot understand how I was so blessed to be born into something so much better, and until this experience, I have never appreciated any of it.

March 17, 2003:

Just before my midnight shift started, the squad was getting ready to go to our assigned OPs. I was gearing up, getting my machine gun ready, and packing ammunition into my rucksack. The alarm horn sounded, and we all started rushing out towards our OPs. As soon as I got outside of our building, I could hear a lot of gunshots. The shots were coming from the east and as much as I wanted to head that way, my OP was on the west. I needed to respond to my point. Just because the compound is taking fire from the east does not mean a second attack is not coming from the west, and we need to secure every inch of the perimeter. Any time there is an attack of any kind, we are required to go to our assigned points and not necessarily where the current attack is located.

The gunshots lasted for maybe forty-five seconds to a minute after I started hearing them, and then they were done. I found out a few minutes later that an OP along the east wall had taken multiple shots from a large, open field across the street from the compound. It was pitch black outside, and no one knows how many people were out there, but rounds did strike the OP. No one was hurt, and even though the guy inside the OP was shooting blindly into the dark, laying down fire from an M249 sent the shooter running. It is just another reminder that anything can happen at any time.

The fact that anything can happen at any time sounds stressful, but to experience it is something completely beyond that. Every night I sit in my OP just hoping not to be hit by a sniper. Every day I patrol the city on foot, and I pray I won't be shot or blown up. Every time I try to sleep, I hope I am not woken up by the warning siren or by an incoming rocket. You cannot become complacent and develop an attitude of "It won't happen to me." That kind of thinking gets people killed; however, it eats you alive to constantly be prepared and worried about what is lurking behind every corner. It is a shit situation with no alternative, and it is a perfect example of being damned if you do and damned if you don't.

I know this place is not only getting to me, I can see it in other people also. Guys that were funny and goofy when we first got here are different now; some are barely talking, and others are just constantly negative about everything. Guys that were friends now seem to hate each other. We all do our jobs every day, and we do them better than could ever be asked of anyone, but it is taking its toll on everyone.

Later on in the night, around three o'clock or so, I heard a single gunshot. It came from the north and sounded like it was right along the north wall. The Sergeant started calling out for someone to advise on the location of the shot, and a patrol group announced that the shot came from inside OP 7, along the north wall.

The Sergeant called out to OP 7, and he was not getting a response. My heart sank, and my stomach just knotted itself right up. The guy assigned to OP 7 tonight has been having a lot of problems here. He has not been adjusting well, and he seems to be absolutely despising every minute of being here. He hates leaving the compound for missions, he hates being alone in the OP, he just hates this place, and this place is just a little more than he can handle. At that moment, I honestly thought he had killed himself.

About a minute later, the Sergeant announced over the radio that he was at OP 7, and everything was fine. As the night went on, the Sergeant went to each OP and told us all that this guy had had an incident; he was okay, but he was probably going to be leaving in the morning. The Sergeant did not offer anything more, and I did not ask for it. I think we can all assume that he came a little too close to doing something very sad, and he needed to be somewhere else. None of us want to be here, but he really needs to be sent home. This guy is sinking fast, and he needs to be pulled out before it is too late.

Last night was a crazy night, and I am very tired now. More of the same old shit went on after shift ended, but nothing worth mentioning. I am ready for a few hours of sleep, and then I have to wake up to do it all over again.

March 18, 2003:

Before we started shift tonight, the squad got some very scary news. Two hours outside of Kabul, in an area where we are always on missions, an American vehicle was hit in a convoy. There were four troops in the vehicle, and it was most likely a Special Forces team. Two of the troops are alive, one is dead, and one is unaccounted for. "Unaccounted for," "missing," "being taken," however you want to word it, it is our worst fear here. I hope he is found soon, but if he does not get out alive, I hope he dies quickly. Being taken by these animals is horrifying. Torture, beatings, and beheadings are almost a complete certainty.

When we are on patrol in the city, we stay together and stay very close. If you become separated from your team and find yourself alone, you might find yourself with a bag over your head and on Al Jazeera for the whole world to see. Inside Camp Eagle, it is fairly safe from this threat as it is in the surrounding area. It is when you leave the relative safety of the city where the real threat comes. Firefights happen every day in the rural areas, and if your team is overrun, you are done. There is just no other way to put it.

Every time we load into an SUV or a HUMVEE and roll past the gate, I think about that tank that stopped us. It happened so quickly that none of us saw the situation coming, and yet it happened. The situation practically appeared from nowhere, and within seconds, we were over our heads in a situation with very few options. I still wonder constantly what their intentions were. I half think that if they were really intending on taking us, they would have. They would not have cared two shits about us calling anything in; they would have just done it. However, that thought does not calm the fear that, even if for just a few moments, they had complete control over my life. The fate of whether I lived or died sat right in their hands, and I was completely powerless to do anything about it. It all happened without the slightest hint of a warning, and could happen again in just the same way.

The rest of the midnight shift in the OP was very quiet, and gave me a lot of time to think about what I just wrote. It is an amazing way to put your life into perspective and realize just how very fragile your existence really is.

March 19, 2003:

The war in Iraq is getting very close to commencing, and things are getting very tense around here. Security is increasing, and rumors of various attacks are flying around Kabul. Attacks against coalition forces have been on the rise lately, but the word is that they are going to start hitting us very hard in pro-Taliban areas. We have also been hearing about thousands of Pakistani trained, pro-Taliban, jihadists crossing the border into Afghanistan to begin attacking American forces. We have been hearing intelligence reports that these jihadists have been training in urban assault and warfare, mountain fighting, and how to use explosives. These rumors do not sit well when I know we are not far from Pakistan, and our compound is right along the main route from Pakistan into the downtown Kabul.

The soldier that went missing yesterday was found this morning and sadly, he was not alive. He was found about a mile away from the point of attack, and they said it looked as though he died fighting. He fought to the very end. As sad as that seems, it beats the shit out of the alternative of being captured.

After shift, we had to go out on a foot patrol in the city. It was the same deal as always, four three-man teams loaded into three trucks. We got to our area and left one team to guard the vehicles while the rest of us broke off to our assigned zones. Today, we were in an area with a lot of shops, shitty little businesses, a lot of cars, and mobs of people. We were assigned to patrol this district because of recent information that this area may be the target of attacks against American interests. We have been to this area many times before and have always found it to be very American-friendly. Most of the stores have signs in English and American flags waiving in their entrances. A lot of the signs try to integrate "American" any chance they get. They use, "American movies," "American Coffee," etcetera. They just want our money; they do not care about us.

Today was eerily different. The American flags are all removed, the signs have absolutely no English anymore, and every hint of American support is gone. This made us all think that the threats may be very real. If the locals are willing to pass on the chance to make a dollar, there is definitely something to worry about. None of them want to be the one store with an American flag in the window. Being the only store showing American support would be just begging to be bombed.

Regardless of the threats, today went very well. No one was hurt and nothing significant happened. Every time a patrol or mission ends, and I safely return to the compound, I just cannot help but feel like I am tempting fate every time I leave.

March 20, 2003:

Tonight was the deadline for Saddam to leave Iraq, and that deadline came at one thirty in the morning, Afghan time. For the last week, we have been receiving more and more reports involving threats to various American interests in Kabul, as the impending war in Iraq looms closer. Since nothing big was actually happening, I assumed it was all bullshit.

Around three o'clock in the morning, it was very quiet in the OP, until the sky lit up with a bright white flash to my east. Seconds later, I heard a massive explosion that shook my entire OP. Within a minute, the north gate reported an orange streak over the compound, traveling towards the east. As he was calling this out on the radio, there was another huge flash and powerful boom to the east. Almost immediately after, I saw two orange streaks followed by another flash and two explosions. The explosions were about a half mile to our east, and they were very powerful.

Situation reports started coming in from other compounds in the area, and I heard that HIG fighters were firing rockets over our compound and towards a compound just blocks from ours. The rockets missed their intended targets, but completely destroyed a shopping district less than one half of a mile from our north gate. Because it was so late at night, there were no fatalities, no American injuries, but several civilian injuries.

After shift, several of us were assigned to patrol the area that was hit by the rocket attack. The impact of the rockets turned about ten buildings into piles of rubble. We were supposed to stop people from looting the shops that had been leveled, but we did not bother to stay very long. Upon our arrival, there was nothing left to protect, and we found everything was either blown apart or burned prior to us getting there. What little had made it through the explosion was probably already stolen throughout the night.

It was a very nerve racking night. It is amazing how a three minute rocket attack can get your adrenaline so jacked up that it takes hours to settle down, and when it finally does, you just crash.

March 21, 2003:

The war in Iraq is in full swing, and bombs are falling all over Baghdad. Ground troops are already fighting in southern Iraq, and we are hearing that there have already been Marines killed in action. I have no idea on any specific details, that is just the little bit that we have heard.

The compound's commander decided to play it safe and had every soldier on the compound assigned to a fighting position tonight. We ended up with nearly triple the normal man-power. The wall was lined with machine gunners, MK19 fully automatic grenade launchers, and AT4 rocket launchers. The night went without a single incident. I think it would take just one look at that wall to realize it was not worth attacking tonight.

Around six thirty in the morning, I was pulled off the wall to go on a mission with the rest of the squad. We were heading out with a team from another unit and two Intel guys. We had no idea where we were going, what we were doing, or what was about to happen. We were just told to get our gear and move our asses. This was really very strange.

The two Intel guys with us were both Americans, but they each had a long beard and wore local civilian style clothes. These are the kind of guys that run around the city, making and keeping contacts, and gather all of the intelligence which we end up hearing in our nightly reports. Always listen to the street because the street never lies, and these guys are listening. It is their job to know who is planning on doing what, and then they are tasked with making sure it never happens.

We rolled out of the compound, and hauled ass through the city. As the driver weaved through the stream of bicycles and shitbox cars, we were finally briefed on our mission. The Intel guy riding in my vehicle told us there was reliable information that a small group of Al Qaeda fighters were stockpiling weapons in a remote village about thirty miles east of Kabul. The obtained information also hints that there may be two high ranking Al Qaeda officers who have been causing a lot of the recent problems in the area.

We were heading to that village to take the Al Qaeda officers into custody and to seize the weapons cache. We were told, "Try to take them alive, but a fight is a fight, and you guys do whatever you have to do. Just try to take them alive."

We got to the village, and we quickly located the Al Qaeda safe house using the information provided by informants. There were very few people milling around, and it seemed as though no one was expecting us. The safe house was a small, two-room shanty wedged between two shops, and it was very easy for us to secure.

The entry team stormed in, and we easily controlled everyone in the room without a fight. There were nine Afghans in the shack, all living off of blankets or makeshift cots. The Intel guys quickly learned that five of the people inside were locals sympathetic to the Taliban's cause. The other four were Al Qaeda members known to the Intel guys.

Right in front of the safe house, the other half of my squad found a piece of crap pickup truck with a tarp thrown over the bed of the truck. They found AK47s, three rocket propelled grenades, five or six rockets, and a lot of ammunition. It was not the mother lode of weapons we were expecting, but it was still a nice find.

Once everything was settled, and everyone was secured and restrained, the Intel guys did their thing and made some phone calls on a portable satellite phone. We were all told to hang tight and secure the people inside. About an hour later, an Afghan National Army (A.N.A.) truck came with an A.N.A. squad.

The A.N.A. squad met with our Intel guys for a few minutes, and they then began taking prisoners out of the safe house. It took them a few minutes to sort out who was who, but they eventually brought seven people out to the trucks and left two of the prisoners in the residence. We were told that the seven prisoners were being taken into custody by the A.N.A. and would be transported to a facility to be interviewed by them. I stayed inside, with two other troops, to watch the two remaining prisoners. After a few minutes, two A.N.A. soldiers came in and gestured for us to leave the shack.

We walked out of the shack, leaving the two prisoners with the two A.N.A. soldiers. Within seconds of walking beyond the door and into the dusty street, I heard a single gunshot, followed by a short yell and a second gunshot which was followed by silence. A moment later, the two Afghan soldiers exited the shack, one still holstering a handgun.

I did not need to go inside to confirm what we all knew. I did not need to see two more bodies. That is one thing I do not write about very often in this journal, but death is constantly around us. Death is a part of life in Afghanistan, and these are just two more dead bodies that I do not really care to see.

I asked the Intel guy why he wanted us to take the two Al Qaeda officers alive if they were just going to be killed. He told me those were his orders and said, "We were just told to take them alive for A.N.A. Once we transfer custody, what they do is up to them," and that was the last that was spoken about it.

Seeing things like this in television or movies is one thing, but when it is right in front of your face, day in and day out, it is something completely different. The part that scares me is I feel like I am growing numb to it all. In the beginning, my stomach used to churn when I saw a dead person, and the results of such violence seemed to haunt me. Now though, it is different. I barely even seem to care. It is almost as if they are not even human to me anymore, and I am not sure where I lost that. I think it is an internal defense to dehumanize these situations to make them easier to deal with.

As we loaded into the vehicles, we left with the sight of a kid, maybe six or seven years old and with both legs missing, trying to hobble his way to our vehicle to get some food or water from us. The driver just drove away, blasting the cloud of dust kicked up by the vehicle towards the little boy. This place is killing me. It is absolutely killing me.

March 22, 2003:

Today marked one month in Afghanistan. The past month seems to have gone by fast and yet dragged by at the same time. It sounds kind of strange, but it is hard to explain. It seems like a milestone, until I stop and realize that I still have months and months to go. When I look at it like that, it feels like I have accomplished almost nothing.

Next door to our compound is a house that is actually quite lavish, at least by Afghan standards. It is the home of a powerful warlord, and although it may seem like a bad neighbor to have, it actually works to our benefit. He is a very powerful person in Kabul, and he has a lot of influence over the local police, A.N.A. soldiers, and other paramilitary groups in the area. I guess it kind of keeps us a little safer knowing that some people may be less likely to attack us in fear that it will piss off the warlord; however, I guess it could also make us a target for rival groups who hate him even more than they hate us. We could just end up in the crossfire.

For the past month that I have been here, I can see that the relationship between us and our illustrious neighbor is less than harmonious. During the day, our compound is usually buzzing with activity and always very loud. Trucks are coming in and out all day, people are constantly yelling, and we are basically shitty neighbors. Any time we play wiffle ball in the rear of the compound, the ball always manages to make its way over the wall and into his yard. From the shit they yell back at us, I can only assume it pisses him off an awful lot.

Early this morning, at the very end of the midnight shift, our neighbor came to the front gate demanding to see the commander about something that pissed him off. The "gate" is not really much of a gate; it is just a short driveway that cuts through the compound with a checkpoint at each end. There is a bar that can be raised at each checkpoint, along with a lot of machineguns.

The Colonel said he was not coming out to meet with the warlord, and he instructed the Sergeant on duty to go in his place. The Sergeant informed our neighbor that the Colonel was not coming, and he became infuriated. He announced that he was coming in anyway, and he proceeded to walk past the first checkpoint. The Sergeant tried cutting in front of him, but the warlord sidestepped and continued to walk. The Sergeant then forced himself in front of the warlord.

Another Sergeant yelled over the radio, "Wood, put your sights on him. If he reaches for anything, touches

Sarge, or gets to that second checkpoint, you fucking drop him."

My M249 was already aimed right at his chest, locked and loaded, with my finger on the trigger. I slowed my breathing down, and watched his hands as he and the Sergeant yelled back and forth. Even though it was no warmer than fifty degrees outside, I could feel a bead of sweat form on my brow.

He was pacing towards the second checkpoint as he was yelling, and he reached a point where I figured he was about five steps from the checkpoint. I decided that would be my decision point, and if he continued any further, I would kill him on the fifth step.

He continued to yell at the Sergeant, and was making a gesture with his hands in which he was smashing the side of his right fist into his left palm. He turned and started walking in what felt like slow motion: one step, two steps, and three steps. As he made the forth step, I began to pull up the slack on my weapon's trigger and gently squeeze in; four steps. I prepared for the fifth step, and he suddenly stopped and yelled "Fuck you, Americans. Fuck you," and he turned and walked away from the gate. As he rounded the corner back toward the street, I released the trigger tension and exhaled deeply.

As soon as the incident with our neighbor ended, I turned around and noticed my morning relief was there, and my shift was over. There were no missions today, so I had a little "me" time to check email, take a shower, and play volleyball with the guys. I hit the gym for a little while, and now I am here writing about my day. If I go to sleep right now, I am actually going to get a good seven hours of sleep before I need to be up again for the next midnight shift. Seven hours of sleep never sounded so good! I hope the next month goes by faster than the past one.

March 23, 2003:

Last night, before shift, a few of us were starting to wake up around ten thirty. I like to sleep all the way until eleven thirty, but some of the guys like to get up early and make something to eat. They were making just enough noise to start waking me up, but not enough to completely wake me.

The Platoon Sergeant stormed into the room yelling for us to gear up and get ready to move. He said a mission came in, and first and second squad needed to be ready to roll out of the compound in ten minutes. He said, "Let's move guys. Full battle gear and all the ammo you can carry." Someone asked about our shift, and he said that the other squads would cover for us.

We all got our gear, and we were upstairs, within a few minutes, waiting to find out where we were going. The Sergeant announced that an American helicopter crashed about thirty miles outside of Kabul, and it was being treated as though it was shot down. The reaction teams at Bagram were already involved in a fire fight to the north, and the weather and high winds at Bagram were also hindering efforts to get helicopters off the ground. An Italian ISAF team was in the area and responded to the crash, and they immediately found themselves taking enemy fire.

I guess there was some confusion about whether or not choppers from Bagram were moving, so we were going to back up the Italians. We loaded up the trucks and prepared to roll out. Just as we were ready to leave, we got the stand down order from Bagram, and we were advised that choppers had been dispatched. Americans were on the ground now, and they felt they had the situation handled. Close calls seem to be the story of my life here!

We all went to our assigned OPs and did the shift without a single incident. By daybreak, the normal traffic was out, and by eight o'clock, the streets were teaming with people. Nothing else happened today that is really worth writing about, so I guess I will call it a day and get another decent sleep. Today was just another day in paradise.

March 24, 2003:

What a shitty, shitty day. I would write about it, but why? Who wants to remember any of this shit anyway? I am going to bed.

March 25, 2003:

The midnight shift was uneventful, as usual. It was a quiet night again, thanks to the rain. After shift, my squad went down to Chicken Street to pick up some things. Chicken Street is a very weird place. It is definitely a shithole, but there are shops where you can actually get some very cool deals. Almost every shop sells bootleg DVDs; some are even movies that are still in theaters in the United States. The asking price is usually two dollars, but you can talk them down to a buck. Sometimes you will get burned, and the movie is nothing more than some guy in the theater with a camcorder, but most are actually pretty good quality. Either way, it is not bad for a dollar.

The dangerous part about Chicken Street is that it is frequented by American troops, and that means two things: from the second you step out of the vehicle, you are swarmed by women and children begging for money, or they are trying to sell you pieces of junk that you do not want. Secondly, it is a very easy and obvious target to attack if you want to hurt Americans. The beggars are very forward and pushy, grabbing at you, crying, and doing anything they can to get your attention. I feel terrible for every one of them, but it creates a very dangerous situation. Don't get me wrong, I feel bad that they live this way, but I am not going to die because of it. One Taliban with a handgun in that crowd, and I would probably never even see it coming. If you shove them aside, and yell at them long enough, they usually realize you are not going to give anything.

Whenever we park the trucks, at least two guys have to stay and watch them to make sure nobody steals from them or straps a bomb underneath. The last thing you want is to drive off and get blown to hell twenty feet down the road. Our simple rule is that we will deal with you bothering us, but nobody touches the vehicles. If someone touches the vehicle they get an M16 in the face fast, and at least one person always tries to open a door even with us standing right there. When that happens, they have two options: they can walk away or be carried away. They know we are not playing around, and they always walk.

There have been a series of "syringe attacks" in Kabul recently. A woman, a man hiding in a burqa, or a child will walk up to a soldier and stick them with a needle. I have no idea what these needles are loaded with, but I sure as hell do not want to find out. They prefer to use the children to do this because they know we are a lot less aggressive with little kids, and they can actually get close enough to touch us.

Another guy and I were watching the vehicles when the beggars came. The trucks were parked along a busy sidewalk, on a street crowded with people, bicycles, donkeys, carts, and pedestrians. The air was so thick with soot and smog it was enough to choke you. I was at the rear of the vehicles, and my buddy took watch at the front.

The beggars came, and the women and children started swarming us. I put my back against the truck and pointed my rifle anytime someone came too close for comfort. It is heartbreaking to point a gun at a kid, but I'm not dying here; I am just not going to let that happen. Having my back against the truck does not give me the best view to see what my buddy has going on up front, but I do not have to look over my shoulder this way.

The beggars usually keep their distance and say things like "please food" or "dollar please." I heard my buddy yelling a few times for someone to get back. They do not speak English and have no idea what we are saying, but a rifle in your face with someone yelling should be a good enough indicator. I heard him yell a few times, and I yelled to see if he was alright. He said he was, but we needed to leave. A woman in a burqa reach for my buddy, and he reacted by smashing the butt of his rifle against her head, dropping her instantly. I did not see it happen, but I saw the traffic instantly stop. People started running toward us and screaming at us. The guys in the nearby shop saw what happened and came rushing out.

The guys had to force their way through the crowd, and people were yelling and spitting on me as I waited for the rest of the guys to get to us. Once we were all at the vehicles and accounted for, we loaded into both vehicles and started inching through the crowd. I wiped the spit from my face, as I could hear rocks hitting the vehicle. Once we broke past the crowd, we were back inside the compound within just a few minutes, and nobody was hurt except for that woman.

Today on Chicken Street was a perfect example of how quickly shit can fall apart here. You can go from calm and stable to completely out of control in a matter of seconds, and once it starts, there is no way of stopping it.

March 26, 2003:

Nothing happened today, and I am tired. Even if something had happened, I do not feel like writing. I am becoming very exhausted; I wish I could take a vacation.

March 27, 2003:

My life in Afghanistan can be summed up in one word: "misery." My job here is to sit in a tiny wooden box, hoping that I don't get shot or blown up. Then I go out on patrol in the city and hope I don't get shot or blown up. Then I go out on missions to the middle of nowhere, hoping I don't get shot or blown up.

It is starting to become like second nature, when a car slows down or stops near me on the street or under my OP at night, I take a breath and pray it does not explode.

Inside the Camp Eagle compound, it is dirty and old, but it is relatively nice. Sometimes it is just nice enough to let me forget where I am for a few minutes; however, one look into the street from the wall is all it takes to remind me exactly where I am. All I see is violence, poverty, and disgust on a daily basis.

Sexual assault on young boys is rampant here, and no one seems to care. Every morning, at the end of shift when the streets are busy, I see scores of young children walking alone in the streets. Some of them are just barely five years old. All too often I will see at least one car stop, with some degenerate getting out and grasping a child's hand, and lead them back into the car. The guy will then drive off with the child, and we all know what is going to happen to them. We are strictly forbidden from interfering in "legal matters" in Afghanistan, and I am supposed to just pretend I do not see what is happening. Some child, practically still a baby, is being driven off to be raped by a pedophile, and I just have to say, "Hey look, it's almost time for breakfast."

This morning, a guy on a bicycle was struck by a car. The traffic was moving slowly, so the bicyclist was not hurt. It was not anything major, but of course it had to turn into a fight. This fight was over almost faster than it started. The bicyclist got off the ground, and stood in front of the car that struck him and began yelling at the driver. The driver got out, and what seemed to be without a second thought, he pointed a handgun at the bicyclist and started firing, with one round clearly striking him in the head. The bicyclist's body dropped dead to the street. He did not go flying back like in the movies; in fact, he didn't move forward or back at all. It looked almost as if his knees and legs just gave out from under him, and he fell straight down.

I raised my M249, and the driver looked up at me as he got back into his vehicle and drove away. I watched him drive off. This guy was shot dead, less than twenty feet in front of me, and all I could do was watch. Unless we are threatened directly, we cannot act. Afghans are allowed to do whatever they please to other Afghans, and as long as they do not pose a direct and immediate threat to us, we have to just watch.

The traffic began to back up as I was announcing the incident over the radio. Another driver got out of his own vehicle, dragged the dead body to the side of the road, and then returned to his vehicle to drive off as if nothing had happened. He dragged the body like it was a tree branch which had fallen, and he had seemingly little regard that it was actually a person who had just been killed.

I am really starting to wonder why I am even writing in this thing anymore. People keep journals to remember things, to relive and share cherished memories, but I do not want to remember any of this. I wish I had a delete button to just erase nearly everything I have seen here. I thought this was going to be something that I would want to keep and remember forever. For me, this experience has evolved itself into anything but that.

March 28, 2003:

Midnight to eight was another long, uneventful night. I spent most of the shift just looking out into the cold darkness and thinking. I was thinking about home, thinking about life, thinking about my dreams, and just thinking about any place but here. I think I wrote before that every day in this place seems to take away another piece of me. It is like I am a wall, and every day takes away another brick. I am starting to wonder how many bricks can be left. How long before one piece too many has been taken away?

I have been absolutely exhausted lately, and I have not slept in days. With the weather getting warmer each day, the temperatures are rising, and there are mice everywhere. Throughout the night in the OP, the mice are running across the floor and over my feet. Any time I try to sleep, they run across me as I lay in bed. I close my eyes and try intently to pretend they are not there, but before long, I will feel one on my pillow or walking across me. Whenever I eat, especially in the OPs, they come out in force. If I put my food down, even for a second, I have to wave my hand to shoo them away from my meal before I continue eating. They are everywhere.

All I did tonight was try to imagine being anywhere but here.

March 29, 2003:

I was at the north gate for the midnight to eight shift, and I got settled in for the night. I had just started eating the dinner I brought with me, and at around twelve thirty, I heard three rapid gunshots. The shots were extremely close. I dropped to the floor and heard another three shots, rapid fire from an automatic weapon. I grabbed my M249 and moved towards the barrier to return fire. As I got to the barrier, there were about fifteen to twenty more rounds fired, and I saw the OP just to my east returning fire.

With virtually no artificial lighting outside of the compound, it was nearly impossible to see more than twenty or thirty feet past the wall. Being in the middle of a city, it is hard to just blindly shoot back. Within seconds of the last rounds being fired by the shooter, a vehicle was revving its engine about a block to the north, and I could just see it for a second as it drove west and out of sight. Approval to exit the compound was initially denied, until about fifteen minutes after the shooter, or shooters, fled the area.

Just after sunrise, a few of us went to look around the area for any signs of where the shooter was. About seventy-five yards north and east of the compound, one of the guys found a pile of 7.62mm shell casings in a narrow alley. These are shell casings from the type of rounds fired by a standard AK47 rifle. The alley runs north and south, and the south end, where the casings were found, has a clear view of the compound. The north end of this same alley is the area from which the vehicle fled. This sounds like useless information to have now that it is over, but whoever is positioned along the north wall will know where to shoot back if the shooter returns.

After shift, there were no missions or patrols today, so I got to go to the gym and relax for a little while. Relaxing here is more of a matter of finding a way to hide and stay out of view. It seems like every time we try to have any kind of fun, such as play volleyball or wiffle ball, someone in charge will feel as though we have "too much time on our hands," and they will find something for us to do. When I do find myself with a little free time, I always try to squirrel away and stay out of sight. If I can stay out of sight, then I am out of mind.

I received a care package from home today and wouldn't you know, still no backpack. I was expecting it in this package, but it was not there. I sent my wife an email to see if she sent it, and I received a reply while I was still at the computer. It said, "No, I sent you a package about a week ago, but I forgot to put the backpack in it. Not to worry, it will be in the next one." What the hell? I need that thing, and it is like pulling teeth trying to get it. I suppose it is not really that important; I am just venting. My day is done, and I'm going to sleep. Midnight will be here again before I know it.

March 30, 2003:

Last night at around ten o'clock, the lights were still off in the room, and all the guys were sleeping. I was half asleep and half awake from a frigging mouse that kept getting in my sleeping bag. I just started to doze back to sleep when I heard an explosion. It was loud and so powerful that it shook my bunk all the way down in the basement of our building. The whole squad jumped out of bed and ran for their gear.

I could hear the other squads coming from their rooms, when someone from upstairs yelled, "Everyone move. South gate just got bombed."

As I was running up the stairs, I heard a second explosion, and it was just as strong as the first. It seemed like everyone simultaneously paused in the stairway, with none of us knowing exactly what we were running into. The pause lasted for only a second, and we kept moving.

I was assigned to an OP along the north wall tonight, so I started running towards my OP. I wasn't even half way there, and there was a third explosion so powerful I felt the ground shake. At this point, it was obvious; the compound was under a rocket attack. I ran to the wall, to try to keep from being exposed as much as possible. During a rocket attack, there is no "safe place," just a safer place. I crouched down and forced myself into the corner of where the wall met the ground, trying to limit the amount of my body which was exposed. We call it, "leaving less meat for the bomb to eat." I was in this position for no more than twenty or thirty seconds when a fourth rocket exploded. I stayed in this spot for about thirty more seconds, and then I ran again to my assigned OP.

Once I got there, everyone in the compound was out and the wall was covered by every type of weapon we had. Everyone was vigilantly watching the streets and the sky, all waiting for another rocket to come in. After a few minutes passed, we realized that was the end of it. Everyone was ordered to stay on duty until around three o'clock in the morning, when the commander gave the all clear to stand down. Everyone went back inside, except for the midnight squad and evening squad, leaving three people at each OP. I set my gear up in the OP and settled in for the rest of the night, and it went by fast having people to talk to. Although the rocket attack was long over, I could not help but stay extremely alert for the rest of the night.

These shootings and rocket attacks always happen at night so the attackers can hide under the cover of darkness. During the day, there are far too many people and security patrols around, and there is always too much going on for them to hide. At night, it is a whole different world here. Security patrols are extremely dangerous at night, and accordingly, they are very rare. There are very few people out at night, and it is much easier to hit and run.

Once daylight came, I found out exactly what had been hit by the rockets. The first rocket hit a large wall directly across from the south gate, ripping a huge hole into the ground. The second rocket hit the German ISAF compound next door. The third and fourth rockets both hit the grounds of an all-girls school that borders the west side of our compound. A storage building on the school's grounds was blasted to shit, and part of the wall that separates the school's yard from our compound was damaged.

Just a few minutes ago, I found out that Intel heard the attack was carried out by the HIG, one of the insurgent groups in the area. The rumor is that this was the first of several attacks planned over the next few weeks; all are going to be aimed at American, German, Italian, and A.N.A. targets in Kabul.

After shift, the squad went on a foot patrol in the streets around the compound. The normal crowds were out, but it was very quiet otherwise. I think last night's attacks even have the civilians on edge. They all live in this area, and I am sure they have to be worried that a poorly aimed rocket could hit their home just as easily as it could hit us. I think it is amazing that these poor people have had to live through this kind of a life for so long. First they had to endure the Soviets, then the Taliban, and now this war. It must seem never-ending for them. I cannot imagine having to live my entire life like this. I cannot even begin imagine it, nor do I want to.

March 31, 2003:

Everyone was nervous going on shift tonight. After what happened the other night, I guess it is to be expected. We were told to remain vigilant, but not to worry too much as it is very unlikely for them to strike two nights in a row. Supposedly, they will wait at least a few nights before their next attack, and they are also likely to target a different location next time.

That information turned out to be completely accurate, and it was a very quiet night. After shift, I was checking my email, and it turns out that the rocket attacks made the news back home. Our families are all worried, so I sent out a few emails to let everyone know I was ok. Once I finished my emails, I cleaned my machinegun and sorted out all of my ammunition.

Sometime around nine o'clock in the morning, we loaded up and took off for the day. The squad went to a firing range outside of the city, and we brought enough weapons, ammunition, and grenades to have fun all day. We got back to the compound around four o'clock in the afternoon, and here I am now. It was not a bad day; it was actually a lot of fun, but now I am tired. Tomorrow after shift, we are scheduled for a mission. It is supposed to be within Kabul, so hopefully it will not be bad.

April 1, 2003:

Goodbye, March and hello, April. It was a very typical night on shift, and nothing eventful took place. I heard a few random gunshots throughout the night, but they were nothing for us to be concerned about. We are all getting really good at estimating the distance and direction of gunshots. In the beginning, we would hear a gunshot, then I would hear one guy saying it came from the west, one guy from the north, one guy saying it was a mile away, and another guy saying it was five hundred feet. Now when we here them, the directions are all reported the same and the distance reports are usually very similar.

I also notice that gunshots do not really seem to worry me anymore. In the beginning, I would hear gunshots and worry about them, but not so much now. I guess anything can become "normal" if it becomes routine.

After shift we went out on a mission, but it was an easy one today. A supply truck needed to go from Bagram to Kabul, and all we had to do was drive out to Bagram and escort them back to Kabul. They usually go this route alone, but yesterday someone shot at an America convoy on the same road. We are better off being safe than sorry, I suppose.

We got out to Bagram to find the supply truck was already waiting for us, so we were back on the road in almost no time. The ride back to Kabul was long and bumpy, but completely uneventful. We were back in Kabul and done by eleven o'clock. It left plenty of time for a good workout in the gym, a decent shower, and time for a good sleep. The mice are still everywhere, but I am getting somewhat used to them. Once I fall asleep, I can sleep through the mice without much bother. That is it for today. It can become very repetitive when each day is almost identical to the last. Maybe, in its own way, that is actually a good thing.

April 2, 2003:

Shift was very quiet again. There are only a few more days before my squad will change shifts. We will be going from the midnight to eight o'clock shift over to the four o'clock in the afternoon to midnight shift. I think that is going to be a lot better for me. There are very rarely missions at night, and I will get to sleep every night after shift. The squad will spend six weeks on that shift before we switch back to midnights for six weeks again. Anything to break up the monotony will be very welcomed.

Sometime in June, this compound is supposed to close, and exactly what that means for us is anybody's guess. We could end up assigned to another compound in Kabul, be transferred to Bagram, or go to another part of Afghanistan all together. There is also the remote possibility we will go home. I doubt that last one will be the case, but I can hope.

Around seven-thirty in the morning, as the end of shift was approaching, an Afghan man walked up to the north gate while carrying a young child in his arms. The boy was maybe seven or eight years old, and he did not look well at all. The child was completely unresponsive, and his ankle was bruised and swollen to the size of a grapefruit. We figured it was broken, and the Afghan guard at our gate told the father we could not help him. A Sergeant with me told the guard to tell the father to take the boy to the Kabul Medical Center.

The Kabul Medical Center is very disappointing for most people. They see well over three hundred visitors per day, and with enough staff, medicine, and supplies to treat only the sickest and most injured, many are turned away without being cared for.

As the Afghan guard was talking to the father, the boy began to vomit and have a seizure, and the father said something to the guard. The guard, who speaks decent English, looked at us and said, "He was stung by a scorpion."

Our compound has limited medical supplies, and although we are not a medical center by any means, we do have a number of doctors on the compound. Camp Eagle serves a lot of purposes and one such purpose is to provide a safe residence for various Americans. We have a few military and non-military doctors, who work at area medical centers during the day, living on the compound.

The Sergeant made the decision to let the boy in, but the father was told to stay outside and just beyond the gate. We radioed to have medics meet us at the gate, and two of the doctors came rushing out. Within seconds, their tone changed, and their actions became frantic. One doctor said the boy was close to death and needed to get to Bagram immediately. The Sergeant grabbed four guys off the wall and told them to get SUVs ready. About ten minutes later, the two SUVs rolled out, with two troops in each truck and both doctors and the child in the lead SUV.

Another doctor who had come out at some point and stayed behind said the child had been stung at least an hour before. He said the child was showing signs of severe anaphylaxis, and his likelihood of survival was very slim.

All day long now, everyone has been on edge about scorpions. There are all sorts of critters running around here. There are mice, huge spiders, mosquitoes with Malaria, some of the strangest bugs I have ever seen, and now the scorpions are waking up.

After shift, it was more of the same by going to the gym, checking my email, and now it is finally time to get some sleep. Tomorrow we have no missions or patrols scheduled, so we are putting together a squad football game. We are going to try to put a game together anyway.

April 3, 2003:

Shift was long and boring tonight; I just sat in the OP and watched the street. From midnight until about six-thirty, not one person went by. I did not see a single car, bicyclist, or anything else. After six-thirty, it picked up and the people started coming out. By seven-thirty, the street was filled with the usual cars, bicycles, people, and donkeys.

Our neighbors, along the south portion of our west wall, are a group of very strange people. They are Iranians, and the house is actually maintained by the Iranian government as a safe house for Iranian agents in Kabul. We know they are there, they know we know they are there, and everybody just minds their own business. I say they are strange because they act very weird around us. We have an OP that looks right into their "yard," and they are always out trying to talk to us. Even though we do not understand a word they are saying, they keep on trying to speak with us. Every morning, at the exact same time every day, someone comes out of their house and empties a bucket of shit in the back yard. Now, I don't mean a bucket of stuff; I literally mean a bucket of shit. I am guessing they either don't have plumbing or they do and just do not use it.

They usually come out and ask us for different things, and they ask by showing us a piece of paper with something written on it. The two things they ask for the most are breakfast cereals and cigarettes. If you give them candy, they act like a bunch of five year-olds. Iranians are not exactly liked in Kabul, so I think they moved in next to an American compound intentionally for the protection. The Iranians are not liked here for a lot of political and religious reasons, but at the end of the day, they do not bother us, and we do not bother them.

Around seven o'clock, this morning, I noticed a guy sitting on the side of the road, directly across from the Iranian house. He was not doing anything, but that is what struck me as strange about him. Of all the people out there, he was the only one not doing anything; he was just sitting on the sidewalk.

At seven-thirty, two guys rode up on bicycles and stopped in front of the Iranian house. Both men got off of their bikes, leaned them up against the Iranians' gate, and then they just walked away. Now, why would two people just lean their bikes against a gate, leave them unattended, and walk away?

I saw one of the Iranians in the back yard and tried to tell him, but he did not speak English. He called to someone inside the house, and a moment later, a man with a long beard and a turban came outside. He spoke English, and I told him what had just happened. The man with the long beard casually walked toward the gate, grabbed one of the bicycles, and threw it into the street. He grabbed the second bicycle and threw it further, almost clearing the street. The bearded man then casually walked back into the house and closed the door. As soon as the bearded man was back inside, the original, suspicious looking, guy jumped on the bicycle in the street and peddled off.

I am not really sure if the bikes were rigged with some type of an explosive, or if they were just a trial run to judge the reaction by us and the Iranians. I did not see anything strapped or attached to either bike, but the whole thing was just weird. It takes a lot of explaining to describe what happened, but it was all over within a minute or two. This place is loaded with some strange shit.

Today, after shift, we had no patrols and no missions. It was in the upper seventies, and the sun was bright. A few of us hit the gym, and then the squad gathered up in the rear parking area for a squad football game. It is easy to get lost in moments like that and forget where you are. It is a really weird feeling when one minute you are dealing with Iranian agents and the possible near bombing of an Iranian safe house, and the next minute you are playing football with your friends.

I think it was yesterday or the day before when I was talking about all the creepy crawly things we have to deal with here. About a week ago, one of the guys on my squad had to shave his head and use some special shampoo because he got lice. We laughed at him and made fun of him for it. Come on, who would not make fun of their friend for that? Well, as the modern proverb goes, karma really is a bitch. Four more of us now have head lice, and I am one of them. We had to get our heads shaved, right down to the skin, and get our own special shampoo. The worst part was when the doctor told me, "Wood, you guys all need to make sure you're showering more. Make a better effort." How fucking embarrassing!

April 4, 2003:

Not a lot happened on shift last night. It was very quiet, and afterwards, we only did a short three hour patrol outside the compound. A few days ago, I got my smallpox vaccine, and it is really kicking the crap out of me. My whole body aches, and every joint is sore. It feels like I have the flu, but without being sick.

I went to one of the doctors to make sure it was normal to feel this way. He told me it was not unusual, and it would pass within a few days. He said he could write me an order for light duty for a day or two, but I told him I would be fine.

As we were finishing, I asked him if he knew anything about the kid who had been stung by the scorpion the other day. He told me the little boy had died. The doc said he died just shortly after arriving in Bagram, and there was nothing anybody could have done. I did not say anything, but I feel like it was at least partially my fault. The Sergeant and I spent so much time trying to turn the boy's father away; I wonder if we wasted the minutes that could have made a difference. If we let him in right away, would he have lived?

When I think about it rationally, I know it is not my fault. The Sergeant and I had no idea what had happened, we had no idea how serious it was, and when we did find out we got help right away. But it is a little boy, and it is hard to think that those minutes might have made a difference. I will never know either way, and that is the hard part.

April 5, 2003:

Last night was my final night on the midnight shift, at least for the next six weeks. Thank God this shift is over; I have not had a decent sleep in weeks. Every day, when my squad finally gets to sleep, it is right when everyone else is coming in for dinner. It is noisy outside, and it is noisy inside. The kitchen and eating area are located directly above our room, and it gets loud at meal time. Then people from other squads will come into our room looking for something. They will turn the light on, find what they need, and then leave with the light still on and the door wide open. Imagine being woken up every thirty minutes all night and every night for weeks on end. The only thing that makes it even worse is to then try falling back to sleep with a mouse running all over you and under your covers. It is extremely exhausting.

I really cannot wait for this deployment to be over. This place is absolutely miserable, and nothing good ever happens. There are only two ways of living life here: we are either extremely bored or something really shitty is happening. There is no middle ground, no in between. I just honestly feel as though the only certainty in Afghanistan is that tomorrow has nothing good to offer. It gets so depressing when you realize you have nothing good to look forward to. The only thing I have to look forward to is finishing this deployment and going home, but that is months and months away. Hopefully things will get better once I start the new shift, but I am not holding my breath.

April 6, 2003:

Today was my first day on the new shift. The day was beautiful, and the evenings here are actually gorgeous. I slept a normal nighttime sleep, and it was so quiet. I loved it!

The weather today was just perfect. The temperature was seventy-five degrees, and throughout the day, there was nothing but sunshine. Around six o'clock in the evening, I climbed to the roof of my OP to sit and watch the sun set behind the mountains. I felt a cool wind blowing across my face and realized that this moment was absolutely amazing. Regardless of what was going on around me, regardless of what I was in the middle of, this moment was flawless.

Not long after the sunset, the day turned into night, the temperature fell, and it became the cold dark night I have grown to know all too well here.

After dark, I climbed back to the roof and looked up at the sky. The stars were absolutely amazing. There are no streetlights or other types of ambient artificial lighting, so you get to see every star in all its glory. I have never seen anything quite like it. I got lost in my own head, just thinking about the vastness and the enormity of what I was looking upon. It made me realize just how small I was, and how insignificant we all are in the grand scheme of things. Tonight, I found an indescribable beauty while in the midst of chaos, and it made me feel as though I have never been so alone.

April 7, 2003:

I had a hard time falling asleep after shift last night; I think my body might need a few days to adjust to sleeping at night again. Once I am adjusted, I think I am going to love this shift. The best part of it is that there are no missions. We still have to do daytime patrols, but no significant missions. My squad has barely enough people to cover the shift, and we are almost never back from a mission by four o'clock. It is looking as though our shift will have us awake, and ready to do patrols for four or five hours, every morning by eight o'clock. We will then have a few hours before shift starts, then shift, and then off to sleep for the night. This is a lot better than before.

I woke up around seven-thirty this morning, and I found that there were no patrols assigned today. My squad has actually been getting very lucky with that lately. A few guys and I decided to throw the football around, go to the gym, and then just hang around and talk. We talked about random, stupid crap, but we mostly talked about home.

Four o'clock brought the start of shift with it, and I was on the east wall again tonight. There were a few random gunshots here and there, but nothing of any major concern to us. Before I knew it, shift was over, and now I am writing this and getting ready for bed.

Most of the guys in the squad get along pretty well, but I can see that all of our relationships are becoming very strained. We all feel the same way about life in this place, and we are all being torn apart in our own way. No one ever talks about how they feel, and it seems to leak out in other ways. I can see guys becoming upset or depressed over the silliest shit. Mail will come, and if someone did not get a package, they will become upset. Sometimes, we will go to dinner and there will be no more sport drinks left, making someone furious. It is always one stupid thing or another setting someone off. It may sound kind of crazy, but that is just the way it is here. When you have absolutely nothing to look forward to, except a stupid sport drink and nothing else, it becomes an enormous letdown when it is not there. Each and every one of us is doing our best to get through this, and we are always there for each other. I guess that is what is really important and not a drink.

April 8, 2003:

Right next door to our compound is a German-run school for young girls. Every day we see the children walking to and from school, and the little girls are all wearing the same uniform. It is a very conservative looking, long, felt-like dress, with a white head scarf covering their hair. The idea of girls getting an education is not well accepted in Afghanistan, and the school is very unpopular with a many local Afghans. Taliban supporters have openly denounced the school and criticized its being.

Just as my squad was getting ready to go on shift, at about three forty-five, I heard three rapid gunshots, right at the gate. They were followed by a quick burst of automatic gunfire. As we got to the gate, I could not believe what I saw, and I do not think I will ever be able to understand it.

A man was lying dead in the street, having just been shot by one of the Afghan guards from our gate. Before he was shot, he walked up to a group of young girls leaving the school, pulled out a handgun, and opened fire. The Afghan guard reacted by firing at the shooter and killing him.

One girl was struck in the stomach, and she was on the ground screaming in pain. Another girl was struck in the side of the head, with her white scarf almost completely red as her lifeless body just laid there. I could see her eyes were wide open, and they looked like she was staring at something far, far away.

Doctors came rushing out, and everyone started trying to help. A large crowd was gathering, but they were almost completely silent, with many praying. By four-thirty, the injured girl had also died, and we were instructed to go to our assigned OPs and go on as normal.

I always love when something like this happens and they tell us, "Go about business as normal."

The whole story is actually a lot longer and with a lot more detail, but this is all I care to write about it. There are other things that I normally would have written, but I guess it does not really matter that I went to the gym or played with a football. What does any of that matter?

April 9, 2003:

Today started off around seven-thirty. I got out of bed, got my gear together, and grabbed a quick breakfast before heading out for our patrol at eight. Because of yesterday's shooting, the patrol assignment for today was all day long, right up until four o'clock.

On the four to midnight shift, the beginning of the shift is very busy. The streets around the compound are packed with people, so if you are in an OP you need to keep your eyes open and watch for everything. If you are on a checkpoint, you are running your ass off dealing with the stream of vehicles and pedestrians coming in and out of the compound. It makes the day fly by, but both of them are really stressful. It is not like working at a fast food restaurant where if you fuck up, somebody does not get their fries. If we screw up here, someone could get shot, or worse, a vehicle with a bomb could make it inside the compound.

If anyone thinks that there are not people out here who are willing to walk up and simply shoot one of us, they are just plain blind. If someone is willing to walk up to a little girl and shoot her in the head, they will do the same to any one of us without a second thought.

Massoud was back on the compound today. He had gone back to his home village for a little while, to take a break from things. We got to talk for a while tonight, and he told me about his home. He said it is a very poor village, but it is also very nice. Massoud said there is no violence where he is from and practically no crime. He described it as a small remote area that has very little interaction from the outside world. He told me that what I see in Kabul is not all of Afghanistan. For his sake, I hope that is the truth. I cannot imagine this poor man having to live like this for the rest of his life. I get to leave; this is his home.

During the shift, we received a situation report that a coalition compound on the other side of Kabul was hit with a rocket. Within minutes of the rocket striking, a car bomb exploded just two blocks away from the same compound. For us on the other hand, it was nice and quiet.

April 10, 2003:

Working on the four to midnight shift provides me the opportunity to meet a lot of interesting people. The compound has been active for about eighteen months, and there are a lot of local Afghan employees who work here throughout the day. There are gardeners, cooks, construction workers, and others, many of whom are starting to pick up English after months of contact with

Americans. The older Afghan workers tend to shy away from us, but the Afghans in their late teens or early twenties love trying to speak English. A lot of them also try very hard to act American.

The more people I meet, the more stories I hear, and many of them are sadder than the last. One kid, I forget his name, is about eighteen years old, and he has been proud of his new baseball hat for the last few days. It is an obvious bootleg of the real brand, and it is also a very poor quality knockoff. He loves it, and we told him it looks great. He told us it was very expensive, and he had been saving for over a month to buy it. I asked him how much it cost him, and he proudly answered, "Two dollars."

I saw the same kid yesterday, but he was not wearing his hat. I asked him where it was, and he just looked down at the ground as he said, "Stole."

We are ordered not to pay the local Afghans any money or give them any donations. It can be a bad thing because if we give to one, it could get out of hand for everyone else. I normally abide by this rule because I know what can happen. Once you give to one, you get swarmed by others, and it can easily grow to a dangerous level very fast. I *normally* abide by this rule.

About an hour after telling me his hat was stolen, I saw this kid walking from the north gate checkpoint. He was alone, and I saw no one else around. I walked towards him, and I raised my index finger to my lips, making the "sshhh" sign, as I handed him two dollars. I just saw him again today, about an hour ago, and he was wearing a new hat.

Many of the people I talk to tell me stories of war, tragedy, death, and loss. Many of the younger workers are orphans, with some having lost their parents when they were just five or six years old. Most of them are still homeless, and they struggle to survive. This is the most heartbreaking thing I have ever experienced.

The day shift is very busy, but nothing of interest seems to happen. All of the gunshots, rockets, and bombings happen at night, and there are not very many missions on this shift. The foot patrols outside of the compound are not too bad anymore either. Most of the things that used to keep me on edge have become less worrisome and far more routine. Maybe I am just getting used to it, but they do not worry me so much anymore. I think I have surrendered to the fact that whatever is going to happen is going to happen. I can be vigilant and I can do the best I can to stay safe, but there is no use in overly worrying about every little thing. It is what it is, and it will be what it will be.

April 11, 2003:

Around ten-thirty tonight, I was sitting in the OP at checkpoint two, and it was very quiet. Out of nowhere, there was a massive boom that shook the whole guard shack. I looked out of the window, to see if I could see anything, because I could tell the explosion was very close. As the radio lit up with activity, there was another massive explosion. I dropped to the ground and as I did, there was another explosion so strong that it shook the guard shack with enough force to knock my water bottle to the floor. Within three or four seconds, there was yet another explosion. I curled into a ball in the corner of the guard shack, as another one hit. I covered my head with my arms, holding my breath in between each explosion, praying I would not be hit as rockets number five, six, and seven exploded over the course of the next minute and a half to two minutes. As each one hit, I prayed it was the last. After the seventh explosion, they finally stopped.

Once the explosions stopped, I just laid still for a minute. I was unsure if it was really over or just a pause before the next round. Our compound just got hammered, and I had no idea how much damage was done or where the rockets actually hit. My only thought was wondering how many of my friends just died.

The compound erupted into activity and everyone was running to man the fighting positions. Throughout the chaos, everyone was also trying to find out what was hit and if there were any injuries or deaths.

We quickly learned that the first explosion was a bomb placed about fifty feet from our gate. Just seconds before the bomb exploded, guards at the north gate saw somebody walking, but it was too dark to see what they were doing. The guard went to grab a portable spotlight, and that is when the bomb detonated.

The remaining explosions were part of a mortar attack that was likely carried out from just a few blocks away. Not a single mortar landed inside of the compound, but their aim was only off by about one hundred and fifty feet. The mortars landed to the south of the compound, just behind the Iranian safe house.

Once again, hours and days of utter boredom sandwiching seconds of pure terror; that is life in Afghanistan.

April 12, 2003:

Last night's bombing left everyone shaken up. My squad ended up being stuck on shift until four in the morning, and I did not get to bed until almost six. I slept for a few hours, and then had to be back up to go out on a patrol outside of the compound. The day has been overall uneventful, and just another typical day here. It is just after nine forty-five at night, and I am on my shift in the OP as I am writing this.

When I was on the midnight shift, I used to write about the previous day, during my shift, to give me something to do to pass the time. Since we changed shifts, I have been writing in here at the very end of the night, just before I go to bed. Tonight though, I am writing early because I made a decision. This will be the last night I write in this thing. I have already written about more than I ever care to remember, and I really do not see a point to it anymore. I am done.

• • •

3

Welcome Back

AFTER READING MY JOURNAL for the first time since it had been written, the memories came rushing back. Some had never faded, but others, more minor details, had managed to crawl into that spot in the back of my mind where they could have remained hidden forever and never given another thought. I sat crouched on the garage floor, tears rolling down my face, remembering those details that had long been forgotten.

Every Day, I had written in that journal until I stopped writing one random day for no specific reason. I originally decided to keep the journal to document and remember what I thought would be the most incredible adventure of my life. Instead, it became page after page of details that I knew I would trade anything to erase from existence. So one day, I just decided to simply stop writing.

Several weeks after I stopped writing, I was injured in Afghanistan and flown home to recover. My injury was not terrible, but it was bad enough that I knew my time in combat was complete. Although my days in Afghanistan were behind me, my next battle was about to begin.

I arrived in Fort Drum, New York about four days after leaving Afghanistan. I was now assigned to a medical recovery battalion for the purpose of recovering and going through physical therapy. My equipment and gear were still with my unit in Afghanistan, and I had only one uniform and one set of boots. My instructions directed me to the battalion's Sergeant Major for assignment and further orders. I wish I could remember his name, but it has long since escaped me.

"Specialist Wood reporting as instructed, Sergeant Major," I announced as I entered his office.

"At ease, Wood. Welcome back home, son."

"Thank you, Sir. It's certainly nice to be back."

The Sergeant Major gave me my next order by saying, "You're going to be assigned to Company A. The First Sergeant there will get you squared away, and he'll make sure you get what you need."

I thanked the Sergeant Major and asked for directions to Company A. The Sergeant Major handed me a map of the base, and he quickly penned a circle around the area where I needed to go. "Head over there, and they'll take care of you."

Thankfully, I was able to get my car from home before reporting to Fort Drum. Having a vehicle on base made life much easier.

I drove through the densely forested areas of Fort Drum, making my way toward my temporary new home. I had the windows down, and I took deep breaths, taking in as much fresh air as possible. The air was clean and smelled so refreshing as it filled my lungs. It was such a stark contrast to the dank air in Afghanistan that I realized I had almost forgotten what clean air even smelled like. My experience at Fort Drum had so far been very simple, and I was optimistic for the future. That is, until I arrived in Company A.

I found Company A to be in the old section of the base. The area is made up of World War II error barracks, which are essentially open bay-style barracks with no private rooms, no private showers, and no private toilets. The bathrooms are one long row of toilets, directly across from one long row of sinks, and two shower nozzles at the end.

I found one barrack with a large plywood sign leaning against the front facing wall. The board had "Company A Office" spray painted on its surface. I entered the makeshift office and introduced myself to the admin soldier, "Hi, I'm Bryan Wood. I was instructed by the Sergeant Major to report here."

"Welcome to Company A," he replied. "The First Sergeant isn't here at the moment, but I'll assign you a barrack and bunk number. First Sergeant will take care of the rest tomorrow."

I was assigned to Barrack 374, bunk 12-Upper. I made my way to Barrack 374 and entered a dilapidated, single story, wooden structure. The inside was lined with fifteen sets of bunk beds on either side, and each set of beds had a small wall locker beside them. The barrack had a musty, foul smell. My first thought was, "This must be a mistake."

A voice called out, "What's up, man? You new?"

I replied, "Yeah. I'm not sure if this is where I'm supposed to be."

"If you're assigned to Barrack 374, you're here." He continued, "I'm Kevin."

I told him my name and stuck my hand out towards his. Kevin was sitting on his bunk and made no motion to move towards my hand. He said, "I'd shake your hand, but you're going to need to come to me," as he glanced at the crutches leaning against his bed.

Kevin's crutches were the kind that attach to your forearms and have a grip nearly half way down the crutch. I leaned towards Kevin to shake hands. Kevin quietly said, "You're going to wish you were back where ever the fuck you came from, soon enough. This shit is horrible."

I looked perplexed, not fully certain how to respond. Kevin told me to go to my bunk if I needed further explanation.

I made my way down the row of bunk beds, until I came to bunk 12. I was assigned to the top bunk, and the bottom bunk was already in use. My bunk mate was sitting on his bunk, almost unaware of me being there. I tossed my bag onto the top bunk and said, "Hey man, looks like we're neighbors."

My bunk mate did not respond. I noticed he was sitting, in an Indian-style position, in his underwear. It was plainly obvious he had urinated himself as the smell was immediate. He just sat and stared forward, in his urine soaked underwear, while picking a scab on his right forearm.

I returned to Kevin and asked, "What the fuck is this?"

Kevin responded, "I warned you, bro. They're mixing people who are back on medicals with people who just went mental. We're all lumped together. He sits there like that all day and only gets up to go eat. I've been here for a month and haven't heard him talk once. There's a lot more like him in here, but he's the worst."

"This can't be right; it has to be a mistake!"

"No mistake, man; this is reality. Just get used to it."

I returned to the Company Office to ask the admin soldier if there were any other bunks available. As I was being told that there were no other open bunks and I'm stuck where I am, a man entered the office. He was a tall man, well over six-foot-three. His uniform was pressed and starched to perfection and his black boots gleamed with polish. He matter-of-factly asked, "Are you Wood, the new guy?"

I saw the rank on his collar and respond, "Yes, First Sergeant."

"Good, step into my office."

I entered the office with the intention of voicing my concern; however, I was quickly ignored and the First Sergeant coldly interrupted, "I'm First Sergeant Redding. A few simple rules: wake up is 0630, breakfast is 0700. All medical appointments and rehab need to be done by 1130 hours and you need to report to your job by 1200. On days with no medical appointments, you're to report to your job by 0745 hours. Any questions?"

Any questions? I had dozens, but I had no idea where to even begin. I asked, "What jobs?"

First Sergeant Redding replied, "Every soldier in my Company will be gainfully employed. I have two spots available, one is in supply and the other is a kitchen detail. The kitchen detail requires a 0330 wake up."

"First Sergeant, I'm here for physical therapy and rehab. I was hurt in Afghanistan," I said hesitantly.

"Yes, I'm fully aware of that. And I'm also fully aware that you are still an enlisted member of the United States Army. I'm also fully aware that every soldier in my company will be gainfully employed. That's twice that I've told you this, and there will not be a third time." First Sergeant Redding then sarcastically asked, "Now are there any other questions?"

I began to ask about the living quarters, but I was quickly interrupted again, "Wood, you were assigned to a barrack and a bunk. You will remain assigned to that barrack and bunk, period. You're dismissed."

I attempted to explain my situation again, but my concerns were quickly cut off with an interruption, "I believe I just told you that you were dismissed. Once again, that's twice and there will not be a third."

I walked off feeling defeated. At that moment, I realized that I would rather be back in Afghanistan than where I was now. I went to dinner at the base dining facility, and I then waited for night to fall; I just wanted to sleep.

After nightfall, I climbed onto my bunk and lay staring at the ceiling for hours. By this time, all of the barrack's occupants had returned from their own daily job assignments and medical appointments. The noise of fifty soldiers rumbled throughout the entire night. Even into the early morning, conversation was constant and there was virtually never a quiet time.

At random points throughout the night, I could hear my bunkmate crying. The smell, the noise, and the tears stirred an anxiety in me that I had not felt since I had left the chaos of Kabul. I closed my eyes in an attempt to sleep, but the only images I could see made staying awake a better option. I felt like I had arrived in my own personal prison.

● ● ●

Morning wake up came, and Kevin quickly made his way over to my bunk. He said, "Hey, man! You have a car right?"

"Yeah, I do," I replied.

"Is there any way I can catch a ride with you to breakfast? I'll show you around if you help me get there.

They have a school bus that comes around for us, but it's a pain in the ass with my legs."

I watched Kevin walk, and I could easily see walking was a struggle for him. He needed my help, and quite frankly, I knew I needed his. Besides, Kevin seemed like a nice enough guy. I did not realize at that moment, but Kevin would eventually become my lifeline through this place, and I would become his.

Kevin and I went to the base dining facility. It is very similar to a large school cafeteria, and the food was actually pretty good. I offered to help Kevin carry his food tray, but he boldly objected, "I can do this myself."

I looked at him strangely and said, "Doesn't quite look that way to me."

Kevin laughingly replied, "Ok, so I can't do this, but I have to learn."

"How about you learn step-by-step, and start today by letting me carry some of that shit?"

Kevin reluctantly agreed. I knew very little of Kevin at this point, but I was already starting to like him. He was a Warrant Officer and obviously very intelligent. When Kevin would speak, he was very well spoken, and he had a well versed vocabulary. I was very curious as to how he was injured, but yet also quite hesitant to ask. We sat at the table and started to eat.

"So, are you going to ask?" Kevin asked in an assuming tone.

I immediately knew what Kevin was referring to, but I played dumb and replied, "Ask what?"

"Are you going to ask me why I walk like I need a telethon?"

"Really? I hardly noticed. I just thought that was your pimp limp!"

"Whatever, asshole. Seriously, if you're curious I'll tell you."

I paused for a moment and told Kevin that if it was too painful to bring up, I did not need to know. Kevin told me, "No, it's too painful to hold in."

I did not yet understand what he meant by that, but I never forgot him saying it. Although I didn't comprehend the full value of that statement, I immediately recognized the feeling it gave me.

Kevin explained, "I'm a helicopter pilot, or I was a helicopter pilot. I'm not sure yet, but I was in Iraq, and we were running a night time medevac rescue. I was pilot, and then there was my co-pilot, the crew, and two injured personnel. We were flying low and fast, and something happened. Shit went bad really fast, and we crashed. I broke both of my femurs, but I was the lucky one. Everyone else was killed in the crash. Can you believe that shit? I'm the only one who survived."

I watched as Kevin continued on with his story. At times, his bottom lip would quiver, his chin would scrunch, and he would have to pause for a moment or two before continuing. A single tear began to roll down his cheek. The tear was quickly wiped away, and Kevin finished, "That's how I wound up here. I go through agonizing therapy every day, and then I go clean the base library for four hours. I eat dinner, hope to fall asleep, and then I wake up to do it all over again. This place is like a punishment, but I have no idea what the fuck I did to deserve any of it."

We finished our breakfast and went about our day. I dropped Kevin off at the library and reported to my own assignment at Supply Distribution. I reported as instructed, and I was greeted by a civilian employee. He was thin and very unkempt. His hair had a greasy sheen, and he had a pungent body odor.

The civilian employee spoke with a thick southern drawl and said, "I'm Mister Woolard. Now listen here, you'll refer to me as Mister Woolard and nothing else. And I don't want to hear no back talk shit either. I tell you boys what to do, and y'all do it; end of story. If you have a problem with that, I just pick up that there phone and call First Sergeant Redding. We'll have your ass cleaning toilets so fast your head'll spin."

I immediately felt my face getting flushed as Woolard continued on. I had to stick my hand in my pocket to conceal the fist I was clinching, and to keep myself from actually using it. My face must have telegraphed my emotions, because Woolard seemed to be able to read exactly what I was thinking.

"You don't like that, do you?" Woolard asked.

"No sir, that's just fine." I replied. I have fought many battles in my life, and I knew, in the long run, I was not going to win here.

"Good, then let's get you to work."

Woolard walked me over to a long, waist-high wooden table. The table, which was four or five feet wide and about twenty-five feet long, was filled end-to-end with hundreds of pairs of combat boots. Woolard pointed to a large transparent trash bag filled with shoelaces and explained my new job.

"What you're gonna do is string up these boots. I know you got a busted wing, but you should be able to do this with one hand just fine. Go ahead and let me know when you get done, and we'll have someone bring you some more," said Woolard. He continued, "You let me know if you need a piss break. Don't just go walking off without telling nobody."

I sat on a wooden stool for a moment and looked at all of the boots. I tried to estimate the number, and I figured it had to be two to three hundred pairs. I was trying to estimate how long it would take me to lace every pair, and I realized it did not matter; as soon as I finished, he would just bring more. It was hard for me to believe that less than two weeks earlier, I was in the middle of combat operations all over Kabul, Afghanistan. I was dealing with everything from combat patrols and dead children, to rocket attacks and car bombs. Now I am here, lacing boots for this asshole. As I started to lace the first pair of boots, I felt as though my soul was being crushed.

After about four hours of lacing boots, I had to go to the bathroom so bad it was beginning to hurt. I could feel my lower back aching from holding it in, but no matter how bad I needed to go, I could not bring myself to ask that man for permission to do something as simple as use the bathroom. I ignored the pain and held it in, along with my pride. I just spent the rest of the day lacing boots and trying to imagine something better, anything that was better than this.

That night, I found myself laying in my bunk, once again wide awake and staring at the dimly lit ceiling. The mood in the barrack was that of pure depression. It was a room filled with injuries and emotional distress. Not a single person wanted to be there, and no one ever signed up for this. Life had suddenly become almost like prison. I felt my eyes begin to well, but I struggled to choke my feelings back. I would not cry; I refused. I would have given anything to have been back in Afghanistan instead of there. Before this moment, I could not have imagined a place I would despise more than Camp Eagle, but here it was.

● ● ●

It did not take long before I fell into a routine. My days became a blur of going to physical therapy and lacing combat boots. Kevin and I started to become very good friends, and we always found ways to make life seem more enjoyable. Although we ate breakfast and lunch on base, we vowed to leave every night for dinner, and a local restaurant became our haven. We would spend hours there some nights, doing anything to avoid going back to the barrack.

One night at the restaurant, we had two girls sitting next to our table. Kevin struggled to make eye contact with them, but they were not playing along. He eventually conceded to the fact they were just not interested. After the girls finished their meals and left the restaurant, our waitress came over to us.

"Hey guys. You know those two girls that were just sitting there? Well, the one in the white tank top really thought you were cute," she said while pointing to Kevin. "She's single and wanted me to give you her number."

The waitress jotted the number on a pad, tore the piece of paper out, and passed the note to Kevin. "Call her, she's a great girl" the waitress said. The note simply read, "Samantha" with a phone number.

"Score!" Kevin said excitedly. "That's how it's done, my man."

I said, "What!?! You didn't even do anything."

"Yeah, well who got the number?"

I told Kevin, "You got lucky!"

Kevin called Samantha, who invited him to go out that night. Kevin asked me, "Bryan, you want to go out with us?"

I told him that I did not think it was a good idea to bring me on his first date. I said, "Just use my car if you want."

Kevin explained, "No it's not that. She said she's going with some friends, and I really don't want to go by myself. Just play wingman for me. Besides, it will get us out of *there* for a while."

And at that, I was convinced. Later in the evening, we met Samantha at a local bar in a town not far from base. Samantha was with two girlfriends, and they seemed like a fun group to hang around with. As the evening went on, the bar filled, and Kevin and I could not help but notice something unusual.

"Man this place is a sausage fest," Kevin pointed out.

"I know! It's all dudes. I'll be back; I'm going to go get a drink," I said.

I approached the bar to order a beer, and I was told by the bartender that the bar did not serve beer. The bartender handed me a drink menu which listed drinks such as "The Dirty Sailor," "The Salty Rim," and "A Slippery Long One." As I looked around the room, I saw four guys dancing in the corner with their shirts off.

"Dude, this is a gay bar" I told Kevin

"I know man, but please don't leave. I honestly think I have a chance with this girl!"

"You owe me big!" I told Kevin.

By one o'clock in the morning, the true awkwardness of the situation had set in. The bar was jam packed with guys. At that point, Kevin and I were practically the only two with our shirts still on, and I had to deal with the onslaught of guy after guy trying to be the one who picked up the straight guy. I wanted to leave so bad, but I knew I couldn't.

Kevin had been having more and more issues with one of his legs, and I think it was obvious to both of us that he stood a substantial chance of losing it. Kevin always kept a great attitude, and he always seemed happy, almost to the point where I wondered how he did it. How can you remain that upbeat with the constant thought of losing your leg hanging over you? I knew that my night may have been very awkward, but Kevin was having fun.

He was with a girl who did not even seem to notice that he was hurt, and I was sure that he was completely forgetting about everything, even if it was only for a little while.

I believe Kevin really tried his best that night, but I hope his ability to fly a helicopter is much better than his dating skill. I do not think his date was nearly as entertained with Kevin as I was, after Kevin's sixth drink caused him to start spitting while he was talking to people. The night eventually ended, and Kevin never did get the almighty second date.

● ● ●

I would like to say that I started to get used to life in the barracks by this point, but I hadn't. My life was basically a mixture of bullshit from Woolard at my job in supply during the day and from First Sergeant Redding whenever he had the chance.

One night a small group of us were sitting in front of the barracks after dinner. It was that moment where day is turning into night, and the sky has a very eerie glow. It was the middle of June, and the weather was just perfect. Four or five of us sitting on lawn chairs, in front of barrack 374, became a usual sight after dinner.

Redding drove by in his car, and upon seeing us, he made a u-turn and pulled alongside the grass next to where we were sitting.

"And just what is going on here?" he asked in his usual condescending voice.

"Just minding our business, First Sergeant." One of the guys responded.

Redding exited his car and stormed towards us. He exploded in a fit of anger, "I know you weren't referring that to me. I KNOW you weren't suggesting I mind my business. Because I have news for all of you; YOU ARE MY BUSINESS!"

Redding started to go off on one of his usual rants when Kevin stood up and said, "And on that, I'm going to bed."

Kevin started walking towards the door to go inside, but he was quickly cut off by Redding. Redding asked, "And just where do you think you're going?"

Kevin said, "I'm tired, my legs hurt, and I want to go to bed. Now if you don't mind..."

There was Redding, all alone and standing up to a guy with two broken legs. We all knew Kevin was not alone; he had a small group of angry men behind him, all of which were getting very close to their breaking point. Not one of us said a word, but we were all thinking the exact same thing, "Just give us a reason. Please, give us just one reason."

Redding stared at the group of us for a moment, and then he reluctantly stepped aside. He may have been an asshole, but I do not think he was an idiot. As Kevin walked inside, Redding glared at the rest of us and said, "If we were back in the zone, I would crush all of you."

Redding always used references to being back in combat. He would talk about his brief time in Iraq and prior missions in Afghanistan, and this always confused us. We are all brothers together; we fought the same war for the same reasons. That being the case, why would someone act like this? Why would you treat one of your brothers like this?

The following morning, Kevin and I went to breakfast in the cafeteria, and we were talking about the previous night's incident involving First Sergeant Redding. It was actually less talking and more pissed-off venting.

"Redding is bullshit. There has to be someone we can go to about this," I said.

Kevin, in his usual calm tone, said, "There isn't, man. This isn't forever, and we just have to deal with it. It is what it is, man."

"Excuse me. I'm sorry to interrupt, but are you talking about First Sergeant Redding from Company A?" asked a man sitting at the table next to us.

This guy was very unassuming looking, and I would almost describe him as kind of nerdy, for lack of a better term. He had thick curly hair and a pair of glasses that were too large for his face. With this stranger being dressed in civilian clothes, we had no idea who we may be talking to. We both paused without offering a reply.

"I'm sorry. I wasn't trying to eavesdrop, but I couldn't help but overhear your conversation." He slid over to our table and continued, "I'm Bernie, Bernie Sanders."

Kevin and I shook hands with Bernie, and it seemed as though neither of us were quite sure what to say next. I asked, "Are you friends with the First Sergeant?"

Bernie laughed and said, "No, not quite. I heard you mention something about the First Sergeant telling you he was in combat. Is that right?"

"Yes, sir. First Sergeant references his time in combat to us sometimes, but it's usually when he's pissed off about something," I said.

"That's funny, because First Sergeant Redding has never been in combat," Bernie stated.

"Excuse me?" Kevin asked.

"Maybe I should introduce myself a little better. I'm Major Bernie Sanders. I am in charge in the 118th Medical Battalion, which includes Company A. So no, I'm not First Sergeant Redding's friend; I'm his boss."

Major Sanders then proceeded to explain that First Sergeant Redding was a member of an Army Reserve unit which was activated for combat duty in Iraq. When Redding's unit was preparing to deploy, he was deemed unfit for combat duty. Redding's unit continued on to Iraq, and Redding was assigned to a Stateside position at Fort Drum. First Sergeant Redding's first assignment was cut short because of his "distinct inability to work well with others," and he was ultimately assigned to Company A.

"So Redding was never in Iraq or Afghanistan?" I asked, almost not believing what I was hearing.

"Not a day, son," replied Major Sanders. "In fact, he has never even served on active duty. Prior to his assignments here at Fort Drum, he has never served any active duty time at all."

I looked at my watch and explained to Major Sanders that Kevin and I were going to be late for our jobs. Major Sanders said, "You two aren't going anywhere. I want to hear everything that's going on over there."

Kevin and I spent the better part of the next hour just talking with Major Sanders. We did not need to fight or argue, and he just listened. Major Sanders only shook his head and occasionally said, "Unbelievable." He listened as we both explained our backgrounds and what brought each of us to Fort Drum.

"Ok, as of immediately there are some changes for you two. Number one, you do not report to First Sergeant Redding any longer; you report directly to me. Second, as you're now reporting to me I'm going to have you reassigned to also work for me. I could use a couple of good guys in my office to help me out. And third, I can't have my two best men living in squalor. I'll see about getting you new barracks, ASAP."

Kevin and I just looked at each other. "What? Excuse me, but are you serious?" I asked.

"I'm very serious, son. Today's Friday, so I will see you Monday morning in my office. I'm in building 1347 on the third floor," said Major Sanders.

"Eight o'clock, sir?"

"Make it ten-thirty, son. No need to rush," replied Major Sanders as he cracked a smile.

● ● ●

Within days, Kevin and I were living in a new barrack and reporting to our new assignment with Major Sanders. The new barrack definitely was not the Hilton, but it was a vast improvement from where we were. The barrack was a three story, modern, cinderblock building, with a bare white-wall interior. Inside, it was divided into multiple rooms and reminded me a lot of a college dorm. Each room had its own shower, own bathroom, and only two people per room. Major Sanders could not get Kevin and I into one room together, but we were in the same building. Kevin was staying on the first floor because of his legs, and I was on the second. My new roommate was a quiet guy who minded his own business, and he definitely did not piss his pants.

Working for Major Sanders was a lot different than working in the Supply Distribution Center. He had us come in around, as he called it, "ten-ish" each morning, and then he usually had us leave by two or three in the afternoon. It is actually difficult to call it working, because we did very little work, if any at all. We formed a fun pattern of going to a local pizza shop each day for lunch, and then goofing off until it was quitting time. My cholesterol levels must have been screaming, but we were enjoying it.

After a few weeks of working with Major Sanders, Kevin and I were really starting to like him. The three of us had a lot in common, and we formed a very unique bond that I have never experienced, before or since. Kevin and I really liked Major Sanders, and we knew he was really starting to like us as well. To this day, I think we each understood what the other had been through in a way that no one else ever will.

Major Sanders rushed into his office one morning, closing the door behind him. Major Sanders' office was fairly large, with a stately, solid wood desk in the middle. Along one wall was a plush leather couch, and the remaining walls were adorned with diplomas, awards, letters, and accolades. A photo on the wall showed Major Sanders with then President Bush, and another depicted the Major shaking hands with Nelson Mandela. It was a very impressive room.

"I have great news for you two! Well, great news for me actually, but I'm going to share it with you guys first," the Major shouted excitedly. He continued, "I'm being promoted! It hasn't been announced officially, but I have good word that I'm being promoted to Lieutenant Colonel at the end of the year!"

I told the Major how I thought it was great news, but Kevin just began to chuckle. The major asked, "You don't think that's great, Kev?"

Kevin, obviously holding back a laugh replied, "No, it's awesome! I'm really excited."

"What? What's so funny?" Major Sanders asked.

Kevin, now barely able to control his laughter, responded, "Dude, you're going to be Colonel Sanders! You're name will be fucking Colonel Sanders! Let's just promote Bryan to Major so you two can be Major Wood and Colonel Sanders!"

The three of us laughed, with Major Sanders giving Kevin a lighthearted slap upside the head and saying, "Real funny, asshole."

"Oh shit, I'm going to be late. I have to get over to my physical therapy appointment," Kevin announced.

I replied, "See you for lunch, dude. Pizza?"

Major Sanders said, "Works for me."

Kevin added, "Me too."

I had some errands of my own to take care of, so I gave Kevin a ride to the medical facility and then went about tending to my business. Two hours later, I got back to Major Sanders' office to meet the guys for lunch. I found the Major's door was closed, with a note taped to it that read, "Bryan, hang around for a minute. I'll be right out."

After waiting for what was actually twenty minutes but felt like hours, I became very curious about what was going on. Kevin was not waiting with me, so I assumed he was in the office with the Major.

The Major's door opened, and I saw he was alone in his office. Have you ever had that strange, sinking feeling in your stomach, where you somehow know that something is wrong? I was having that feeling right then.

"Bryan, come on in, bud."

"What's going on? Is everything ok?" I anxiously asked.

"No, buddy, it's not."

There was a long pause before the Major continued, "This morning, after you dropped him off, Kevin was in his physical therapy session, and he re-broke his leg. His leg just broke."

"Where is he?" I demanded to know. "I want to go see him."

"Bryan, that's not something they can take care of here. He was transported to the local hospital, and he's going to be transported to another medical center tonight for surgery."

I had no idea where they were about to take my friend, but I wanted to see him before he left. I felt as though I just had to. I asked Major Sanders if I could go to the hospital to see Kevin.

"Bryan, we can't. They're prepping him to be flown out right now. I tried to arrange to have you see him at the airfield before he goes, but it's a no-go."

The conversation continued on like this for quite a while, pleading with Major Sanders until I finally realized I was not going to see Kevin before he left.

Little did I realize that when I gave Kevin a ride that morning, it was going to be the last time I would ever see my friend. Then, just like that, Kevin was gone.

● ● ●

As the weeks rolled on without Kevin, life went on like it always does. I thanked God every night that we found Major Sanders before Kevin had to leave, because I knew I could not have made it through my old situation alone. Life may kick us in the balls, and really hard at times, but I also believe life will always help you back up

127

to your feet and just when you need it the most. I think Major Sanders knew that I was taking it all very hard, and he was always there for me. He became one of the truest friends I have ever had.

One morning out of the blue, Major Sanders called me into his office.

"Bryan," he said, "the only thing that is going to be worse than seeing Kevin leave will be seeing you go, too."

"Go where, sir?"

"Home, son. Your unit is loading up, back in Afghanistan, as we speak. They're coming back, and you're going home."

I had very recently finished all of my physical therapy, and I was medically cleared. At this point, I was simply waiting for my unit to come back from Afghanistan so I could be released from active duty with them.

"When? When can I leave?" I anxiously asked.

"I received an email from your company commander in Afghanistan, and as of eleven o'clock last night they were in the process of loading their equipment onto transport aircraft."

"But when? When can I leave?" I repeated.

"Your unit should be wheels up sometime tonight or tomorrow, and they should have their boots on the ground here in a day or two. After that, I'd imagine you'll be heading home within a week or so."

I asked Major Sanders if he was joking. I begged him not to joke about this.

Major Sanders said, "I'm not joking, kid. That's it; it's all over. You're really going home."

I told Major Sanders, "Thank you, Bernie. I don't think I can ever repay you for what you did for me here."

"Go home, have fun, and enjoy your life. You've been through enough bullshit. Just go enjoy, and make the best out of everything."

I replied, "I will. I really hope nothing but the best for you, and if I ever need a good fried chicken recipe, I'll be sure to call you, Colonel Sanders."

Major Sanders gave me a hug and said, "I'm just glad I was here for you guys."

"I don't think you'll ever know how much you really did for me," I told him.

Exactly eight days after having that conversation, I was home, and the entire nightmare was finally over. I had been so consumed by the challenges of life in Fort Drum that I didn't even realize, but I was quickly going see, that the person I was before this all started had somehow changed. The way I saw the world was gone, and I saw things, almost everything, in an entirely different way. It was now time to face this fact, and I needed to adjust to life in an entirely new reality.

● ● ●

Bryan A. Wood

4

A New Reality

I AM ALL ALONE in a desert, wearing my Army uniform with full battle gear. I'm on my knees, with my fingers clasped and my hands behind my head. My pulse is racing, and I'm sweating so profusely that my uniform is soaked. I don't see or hear anyone else, but I can sense them standing behind me. I can feel that their intentions are frightening, and I begin to panic. I'm instantly laid out on my stomach, with someone's foot on the back of my neck. My face is being pressed into the hot sand, with the grains scraping like sandpaper. I still cannot see who is there, but I can now hear them. I hear them talking about taking me alive, and a bag is slid over my head. The fear becomes so intense that I can feel myself wanting to vomit. I am powerless and cannot move. I can only think to myself that this cannot be happening; it cannot be real.

The dream suddenly ends, and I instantly jolt out of my sleep. I sit upright and panic, not knowing exactly where I am. It takes me a minute to realize it's only a dream, at which point I'm dripping in sweat with my heart pounding.

"Are you ok?" I'm asked by my wife.

I unconvincingly respond, "I'm fine, go back to sleep."

"Ok, just wake me up if you need me," she said.

She rolled to her side of the bed and went back to sleep. I laid back down, and as I'd done almost every night for as long as I cared to remember, I laid awake, staring at the ceiling once again. I thought repeatedly about my dream and could not escape the fear it produced. All I had at that moment was the thought of that dream racing through my mind.

I began having this same nightmare haunt me almost every night. Even while awake, I was not immune from the images and memories that worked their way into my thoughts. Any time I closed my eyes, I could see the image of a young boy lying dead in a gutter. I could instantly see his starved body, and I could hear his mother's cry after she was shoved to the ground. I would feel my heart rate climb, and I would have a sinking feeling in my stomach, as if these experiences were really happening again. Before long, I started to become angry at myself for reliving these moments and allowing these memories to dominate my consciousness. It's my head, I control what goes on inside, and I control what I think. I asked myself constantly, "Why can't I just stop remembering these things?" The harder I fought to make the memories stop, the more frequently they came, and the more memories they brought with them.

I routinely thought about the death I had seen, but the images of poverty and suffering were killing me inside. The memories of people starving, the look on a dead man's face capturing the fear and torment he experienced moments before his death, and other vile recollections were constantly there. The worst were the memories of seeing innocent children, as young as four or five years old, being led off to be what I know was raped by an adult man, all while I was forced to watch and do nothing. Knowing that I watched and did nothing was now pure torture – pure and agonizing torture.

These were the thoughts that swarmed through my head at their own will, leaving me with no ability to control them. My thoughts of these memories were beginning to dominate nearly every waking moment of my life.

● ● ●

My first days at home were somewhat strange. Everything was exactly as I had left it, but somehow it no longer felt the same. When I first got back to my tiny, one-bedroom apartment, I found the television was right where I had last watched it, the couch was right where I had last sat on it, and my bed was right where I had last slept on it. Everything was exactly the same, but it felt as though it all belonged to someone else. It seemed as though I was stepping into someone else's life, and at any moment someone was going to pull the rug out from under me to send me back to some terrible place.

I originally joined the military in 1996, and I got out in 1999. Shortly after September 11, 2001, and once the war in Afghanistan erupted, I learned that the unit in which I had served was being placed at the top of the list for deployment to Afghanistan. I could not help but feel the obligation to my unit, and I felt a duty: if my unit needed to go, then I would need to go with them. I signed a one year contract, essentially agreeing to serve one tour in Afghanistan. What that meant for me, in the end, was once I was released from Fort Drum, I was simply done. I was able to just walk away from the military and return to the life I had prior to signing that one-year contract. I went from the middle of a war to the experience of Fort Drum and then right back home. There was never any buffer between any of them, and I found next to nothing to help me with the transition.

For many soldiers, it was much worse. They were in Afghanistan one day and back in their own living room less than two weeks later. It is so difficult to just turn that "combat mode" off and jump from one extreme to another. Going from war to everyday life turned out to be much more complicated than it was for me to go from everyday life to war. I searched desperately for the metaphorical light switch that would just turn that part of my life off for good, but such a switch simply doesn't exist.

My very first night at home, my family got together at my parents' house, and we all had dinner. We decided on Chinese take-out, and we ordered almost everything available on the menu. We sat around the table, enjoying one another and talking over our Lo Mein noodles and fried rice. I found the conversation mostly centered on Afghanistan and what kind of things had happened there. I told my family about Massoud and some of the interesting things I had seen, but I did not want to talk about anything in great detail.

My father and I were never the touchy-feely, "I love you" types, but we have both always had our own way of making sure the other knew exactly how we felt. I'll never forget the look on my father's face as he talked with me over dinner that night. He was grinning from ear to ear, and he could not stop smiling.

When I was leaving for Afghanistan, I was preparing to board a bus that was taking my unit to mobilization. This was the last time we could see our families before departing for war. As I prepared to board the bus, my father grabbed me and hugged me tighter than I'd ever been hugged. As he squeezed, he whispered in my ear, "I love you, and I need you to come home. So you do whatever you have to do over there, but you come home."

As I looked at my father smiling over his Chinese food, I knew I had done what he asked of me. I could see that he was proud, but more than anything I knew he was relieved beyond words that I had come home. The night drew on, but I still remember how his smile never faded.

The following day, my phone rang, and I answered, "Hello."

"Woody, you're home! It's me, Sean."

Sean was one of my best friends, and before leaving for Afghanistan, he promised me the time of my life when I came home.

"Tonight, we're taking you out, dude." Sean said.

"I don't know, man. I think I might want a few days to settle in, so I can kind of adjust to everything."

Sean responded, "Bullshit, you can adjust with a stripper's tits in your face! We're picking you up at eight-thirty."

I wasn't in the mood to go out yet; I really did want some alone time. I knew though that arguing with Sean would be a fruitless effort, and I conceded to the fact I had to go.

HONK! HONK! HONK!

I heard the repeated blasting of a horn in front of the house. I looked at my watch and saw it was eight twenty-five. I went down to find Sean and another friend, Steve, waiting in the car for me. I got in the front passenger side, and we drove off into the night.

Sean was driving and he asked, "Are you ready for one hell of a night? I'm not drinking a drop, so it's all you!"

"Look man, I really want to hang out tonight, but let's just keep it low key. I'm not up for a crazy night. Let's just all go somewhere, have a few beers, and shoot the shit."

Without hesitation Sean said, "You're the boss tonight."

Sean drove us to the Blackthorne Tavern, our favorite pub. It was a small Irish style pub with dim lighting, low ceilings, and an enormous selection of beer. Located in Easton, Massachusetts, the Blackthorne was very popular with the local working-class Irish.

Sean brought the first round of beers to our table and we began talking the night away. My friends repeatedly asked me what Afghanistan was like, and I vaguely answered, "It sucked," or some variation of that, each time. My friends prodded for stories, but that was the last thing I wanted to talk about. Eventually I was able to change the conversation to other topics, and Afghanistan was forgotten, at least for a little while.

Steve unexpectedly stood up and yelled to the pub's other patrons, "Hey everyone, listen up. My boy here just came back from Afghanistan, and we want to show him a fun night!"

The room clapped and a few people whistled. I told Steve to sit down, because I really didn't want this. Inevitably people in the bar began bringing me a beer, or a handshake, or a "thank you." I pretended to be grateful for each, but I really didn't want them. I didn't want anything from anyone, and I really just wanted to be left alone. This was something that I really did not want; I did not want this kind of attention.

The three of us sat around our small table, talking and drinking. As I expected it to, the conversation shifted back to Afghanistan.

Steve asked "So come on, tell us. How many of those fucks did you kill over there?"

"What fucks?" I asked.

"Come on, dude. You know, those Afghanistan fucks."

I was able to successfully stop their earlier attempts at this type of conversation, but this time I was drunk and didn't have the same perspective. For the first time, I felt like I was beginning to lose control.

"Exactly what 'fucks' are you talking about?" I asked with a tone of anger.

Steve said, "Forget it, man. I'm sorry I said that."

"No. Too late, shithead," I said. I loudly continued, "You're going to tell me exactly what 'fucks' you're talking about."

The area around us quieted, and everyone was looking toward our table. Steve quietly said, "Dude, calm down. I don't want to talk about this anymore."

I slammed the beer bottle in my hand to the table top. I yelled, "No, you wanted to talk about this and here you go. I'll tell you when you're fucking done."

The room came to a dead silence as months of anger came pouring out at that very moment. None of it was Steve's fault, but it came out on him. I looked around the room, and I saw everyone staring at me.

"Fuck all of you," I said as I walked away from my table and out of the door. As I reached the parking lot in front of the pub, Steve came out also and walked toward me.

"Bryan, I'm sorry. That was a dick move in there. I never should have asked you something like that. Come back inside, man. Please?"

Steve and I talked for a minute, and I apologized to him for the way I had acted. We made our way back toward the door when Sean came out also.

"They kicked us out." Sean said. "Your first night back and you already got us kicked out of somewhere. That's why I love you, man!"

"I'm sorry guys," I said. I continued, "I'm just not ready for this yet. I just need some time to get used to being back and dealing with everything. This isn't easy."

Sean replied, "Hey, better here than yelling at some innocent, impressionable, young stripper." He continued, "Come on, let's get you home."

My friends took me home, and the twenty-minute ride seemed to last all night. We tried making small conversation in the car, but it just felt weird and forced. As Sean was driving, all I could think was that I wished I could hang out with Kevin again. Being friends was so much easier with him. I did not need to explain or describe anything to him, and he did not have to explain anything to me. Kevin and I each had different experiences, and his hurt was different than my hurt, but as I would later learn, hurt is hurt. More than anything else, I missed my friend.

• • •

I took the next two weeks off before going back to work. I honestly do not remember how I spent those two weeks, but I do remember eating a lot of pizza and watching a lot of television. I was very eager to get back to my old life, rebuild my old routines, and just get things back to exactly where they used to be.

My first day back at work was basically as I had expected it to be. I worked as the Marketing Manager for a small company, and with only twenty-three employees including myself, they were excited to have me back. I arrived to work a few minutes early, and I found everyone else already there as well. My co-workers were setting up a small party to welcome me back to the office.

One of my bosses, James, approached me and welcomed me back.

"Hey buddy, it's good to have you back!"

I replied, "Thanks James, it's good to be back. It's very good to be back."

"Listen, take your time and get adjusted before you dive into anything. We have a lot going on and I want to make sure you're back in the game before we start dumping things on you," James said reassuringly.

I told James, "No, I don't want to take any time. The more I sit around, the longer it's going to take. I just want to get to work."

"Well alright then, buddy. We have a meeting today at one, and we will get you up to speed and get you assigned to some projects."

I always enjoyed my job, and I knew my return would be welcoming. The company owner, Adam, invited me to talk in his office.

"Bryan, come in and sit down." Adam said.

Adam's office was very large, but always seemed strangely empty. I guess you could say Adam was the typical small business owner in that he was a very nice guy, but he was also very opinionated. Work always had a feeling of Adam's way or the highway, but after all, it was his company. The easiest way to get along there was to just go with the flow and agree with everything.

"Well, let me start off by saying that I can't begin to tell you how happy I am that you're back, and I'm very glad that you're back in one piece."

I said, "Thanks Adam, I really appreciate that."

Adam asked, "Is it as bad over there as they make it out to be on the news?"

I replied, "It has its days. Some days weren't so bad, and other days weren't so good."

"No shit, I bet." Adam said. After a pause, Adam continued, "Bunch of god damn animals."

The conversation was beginning to have the same tone as my night out at the bar. The only difference this time being that this conversation was with my boss. I bit my tongue, and I chose my words with a much greater sense of respect.

"I guess it just depends on how you look at it," I told Adam.

He asked, "What do you mean?"

"It just depends from which side you look at something. I see things one way, and someone else may see them completely different, even though we're looking at the same thing. War is just perspective, and it's only from which angle you're looking that determines your opinions."

Adam said, "War is nothing but a battle of will. It is nothing more and nothing less. These animals have no value for life, so how do you defeat that kind of will?"

I said, "I guess you're right. I have no idea."

Although I answered with an agreement, I could not help but think how ludicrous this was. Who was he to lecture me about the realities of war? I knew he meant well, and that was all that allowed me to agree with what he was saying. The conversation ended, and I returned to my desk to start getting to work.

James came to my desk and said, "Hey buddy, I think you'll like this."

James then handed me a piece of paper. It had a border printed around the edges similar to a design from a diploma or certificate. The title printed across the top read, "Taliban Hunting Permit," in bold lettering, and the remainder of the print continued with something about killing Taliban and Afghan people. The bottom of the sheet had another bold print which read, "Proudly Presented to Bryan Wood."

James laughed and said, "I made that for you, man."

James gave me a pat on the back and walked away. I sat for a minute looking at the paper and simply thinking, "Are you serious?"

I turned my computer on and spent the next few hours poring through the endless backlog of emails I had waiting for me. I started placing personal items back around my desk, and I just worked on getting settled back in. I started looking through the work files placed on a network drive available to all employees, trying to find a purpose to any of them. Strangely, I could not find a single one that seemed to matter. I started thinking, "What was the point to any of this?" It all seemed so irrelevant.

As the day went on, I was eventually in the one o'clock meeting where, thankfully, the conversation was not at all about me. The meeting lasted for nearly three hours, with everyone carrying on about expense reports, spending budgets, quarterly profits, and so on. As each person in the meeting took their turn complaining about whatever issue they were having, I felt more and more cynical about everything. I couldn't believe the things people were complaining about. I also couldn't believe the kind of silly bullshit these people thought mattered in life. More than anything else, I couldn't believe I once thought these same things were important. Now, expense reports were one of the most unimportant things in the world to me. At one point, James said if profits did not increase we could all end up starving on the streets. I do not think James, or anyone else in that room, had the slightest clue what it was like to see someone starving on the street. To them, it was a figure of speech and certainly not something that really happens.

It did not take long before I realized that being a Marketing Manager was no longer the place for me. I did my best to do a great job at work, but it was just obvious I needed to find something new.

• • •

Life was no longer the same. Home did not feel like home anymore, I was forcing wedges between me and my oldest friends, and work became an enormous waste of time with people whom I had nothing in common with. My life became very stagnant, and I lived this way for about a year. I eventually reached a point where I decided I needed to make a change.

About a year after I returned home, I began applying with police departments in Florida. I knew that as a police officer I would be around other people who had seen the harder side of life. I would be around people who would see life in a manner much more similar to the way I did. I also knew it would be in a new environment, with new people, and it was the fresh start I needed.

I went to my father and asked, "Hey Dad, can I talk to you about something?"

"Yeah," he said. "What's up?"

"I'm thinking about leaving. I'm thinking about moving to Florida"

He asked, "I'm not saying it's a bad thing, but why?"

I began to explain the way I had felt, and what my life had been like for the last year. I told my father that I needed a change and how I thought this was something I needed to do.

He explained, "I wish you would do something safer, but I understand. You see life through a very different perspective than a lot of other people now, and you need to go do whatever makes you happy. No matter what you decide to do, I'll always be behind you, one hundred percent."

It did not take long at all until I was offered a position as a police officer with a great agency along Florida's Gulf Coast, and I relocated to a new beginning. Such a drastic change did not come without uncertainty. As I was making this change, I constantly wondered if I was doing something positive or making the worst mistake of my life. I set my fears aside, packed everything I owned into the back of my car, and I went for it. I will never forget my first day in the police academy, and when I realized I made one of the best decisions possible.

There were approximately fifty or so students in the police academy class on the first day, and everyone was waiting anxiously in their assigned seat in the classroom. A minute or two after eight o'clock in the morning, a short, stocky man, in his mid-thirties, walked into the room. He was wearing black shorts with a red, long sleeve tee shirt, with "Instructor" printed in white lettering on the front and back.

He calmly and confidently said, "I'm Lead Instructor Richard Toffling. I'll be leading you and molding you, hopefully into successful police officers. I am going to tell all of you something right now; not all of you are going to make it."

The tone of the room was somber and filled with anxiety and nervousness.

Toffling continued, "To see what I have to work with, I want to go around the room and have each of you introduce yourself to me and the rest of the class. Tell me who you are, where you are from, what you did before coming here, and why you want to be a cop."

The questions seemed simple enough, but that proved to be anything but the case. Each person was criticized for the answers they provided. Toffling managed to find something wrong with the information they gave, no matter what the student said. Each student seemed to feel belittled by the time Toffling was done with them and had them take their seat.

As it came to my turn, Toffling had to squint his eyes to read the name tag on my desk. "Bryan Wood, please stand up and tell us all about you."

I stood up and said, "I'm Bryan Wood, from Taunton, Massachusetts. Before coming here, I was in the Army, and I'm a combat veteran with a rated disability. During my time in combat, I was awarded the…"

Toffling interrupted, "Where did you fight?"

"Eastern Afghanistan, sir."

Toffling calmly and politely said, "Thank you, and sit down."

I asked, "Is that all, sir?"

"Yes, that's all. You can sit down."

It was that very moment that I knew I made the right decision, and I had moved my life into a very positive direction. The remainder of the police academy was very easy, and I ultimately finished first in my class.

I excelled at my new career, and I loved what I was doing. Just as important, I loved where I was doing it. All was not perfect, but life was getting better.

I thought about Afghanistan almost every day. Every time I closed my eyes, I still saw images I wished would have faded but hadn't. My nightmares still attacked me two or three times each week. Sometimes I would wake up, and the dream would end quickly; other times, it would go on until I woke up panicked and sweating.

No matter how my problems lingered, I became a master at hiding them. I learned to hide everything with laughter and sarcasm. I realized that it is hard to suffer when you are laughing, and I basically treated everything in life as if it were a joke. Being a smartass became the medicine that made life much easier to deal with.

I worked hard to take everything day-by-day and just one step at a time. Whether my efforts to this point were a permanent solution, or just a temporary bandage, remained to be seen. For the time being, they were working, and I was getting through life. I managed to deal with every bad emotion from Afghanistan, and I bottled them away in a place that allowed me to forget them. They were bottled away so I could deal with them some other day.

The next two years of my life continued on almost uneventfully. I had sad days, and I had happy days, just as all people do. I was living my life, and I was enjoying my life as best as I could. I thought I had found the answers, but I now know that hiding your emotions behind a mask, and bottling your feelings away, is only a temporary solution. It was only a bandage covering a much greater problem, and sooner or later, bandages will fail and old wounds will bleed once more.

• • •

Bryan A. Wood

5

Falling Apart

TO SAY THE NEXT two years of my life were uneventful would be fairly accurate. I had grown into new habits, I developed new routines, and work kept me very busy. The best part of my new career was being surrounded by people who had a keen sense of tragedy. I worked with people who had experienced and witnessed suffering first-hand and on a very regular basis. There was no arguing about petty expense reports, people prying for gory details about war, or anything else that I had dealt with in the past. It also felt very good to be in a position to actually help people, and I was making a difference in the lives of others.

All this is not to say that there were not problems. Throughout these two years, the recurring nightmares continued off and on. The images persisted, but they gradually began to fade. Strangely, not a day went by where I did not think about Afghanistan in one way or another. As I mentioned earlier, I had done an excellent job holding my emotions and feelings back to this point, but the metaphorical dam was set to burst.

Over the course of the previous year, I had become increasingly frustrated with my wife. This story is not about her, and I am not going to go into great detail about this aspect of my life; however, my marriage was a catalyst for future changes, and it is important to explain.

My wife had become very distant from me in many ways, and she often felt very cold and somehow disconnected from our relationship. I would routinely confront this which would temporarily fix things, but the cold feeling would always return very quickly. This began a cycle of routine fighting and arguing with very little resolution. It bordered on impossible for me to get my wife to enjoy any time with me at home. It got to a point where any time we did spend together felt forced or unwilling on her part.

This distancing manifested itself into numerous problems and breakdowns in our relationship. I watched as my marriage slipped deeper and deeper into disrepair, until it seemed as though it was a struggle for me to continue. One night, everything came to a head.

She said, "I'm going out with some friends tonight. I shouldn't be home too late."

"What do you mean 'going out with friends?'" I asked. I reminded her, "We were supposed to hang out tonight, just us."

"Oh yeah, about that; we'll just plan again for another night."

I asked, "You and I will plan for another night, or you and your friends?"

"Me and you; we'll just do something next week."

I was going back to my days on at work, and since I worked the evening shift, it would be days until we saw one another again.

I said, "Sometimes, I honestly think you couldn't give a shit about us."

This statement erupted into a back and forth battle until I just stopped, and I started thinking. I instantly recalled every step of the last two years. I remembered being back in Afghanistan and asking her to send me pictures of things from home, things to remind me of happy times, and getting none. I remembered begging her to send me a black backpack to carry extra ammunition, and it never coming. I thought about the care packages I received with nothing extra in them to brighten my day. I remembered all of the emails I received with very few sent to see how I was doing, and instead only asking for a PIN number, a password, or how to do something. I recalled all of the nights I woke up from a nightmare in a dripping sweat, only to have her roll over and never speak a word of it. All of these things, and more, came rushing to me when I heard her finally say what I had suspected for some time.

She looked at me and said, "I don't love you. I mean I love you, but not like I should. I don't look at you as my husband, you're just my friend. I haven't been attracted to you in a long time, but I just don't know what to do about it."

The fight calmed, and we talked about our problems. As much as it hurt to hear, I knew that it needed to be talked through. Initially, it was treated as a downswing in our relationship, and we thought it was something we could work through. In reality, the same issue surfaced over and over again, and it became painfully obvious that my staying in this marriage was a fool's errand.

Over the next several months, my wife would have periods where she would make an effort and try to make things better, but as quickly as these times would come, they would quickly pass, and we would be back at square one. This cycle repeated itself numerous times as I painfully watched my marriage wither before my eyes.

● ● ●

Kevin and I had maintained contact through email since he left Fort Drum. Over the last year our emails had become fewer and fewer, and by this point, we barely wrote at all. In every email we would send to one another, we would talk about taking a trip to get together at some point and catching up. We would both agree we needed to do so soon, but life always got in the way, and it never happened. Kevin would usually write and update me on his progress, and he would let me know how he was healing. Over the last year and a half, he had been doing very well and made a lot of progress.

One day I was looking through my email when a new message from Kevin appeared, "You've got mail." This email will haunt me forever.

Kevin wrote, "Hey Bryan! I hope you're doing well. It's been a long time since Fort Drum. It feels like it's been forever since we were there. Do you ever talk to Bernie? Last time I emailed him, he was doing awesome. Good for him!

"The reason why I'm writing to you is to let you know that something happened. I've been having a lot of problems with my left leg and it just never really healed properly. About a month ago, I had another surgery to adjust one of the rods that was placed in my thigh bone. After the surgery, a really bad infection set in. The doctors did everything they could to treat the infection, but it wasn't helping. Last week, my doctor and I decided that it was time to throw in the towel and take my leg. On Thursday morning they amputated my leg just above the knee…."

Kevin's email continued on, but I could barely read it. My stomach sank, and my heart was broken. I always knew in the back of my mind that this day was coming, but I just could not believe Kevin lost his leg. He had been through so much, and he fought so hard, only to lose after all this time.

I am not sure if it was the stress in my marriage that worsened the pain, but Kevin's news bothered me deeply. It not only brought back feelings of pain and tragedy that I had not felt in a long time, but it brought them back with a magnitude that is indescribable. The feelings and pain that had been bottled up for so long were ready to explode, and in an instant, the temporary emotional bandages and facades were no longer working.

The days, weeks, and months that followed sent me deeper and deeper into a dark period of depression. Like always, I tried my best to hide it, but it was always there, worsening with each day. Work became a disinteresting chore, and I began to distance myself further and further from friends and family. I painted myself into that proverbial corner where I felt I had nowhere to go, and I felt I had no one who could ever understand me. I felt as though explaining all of this to someone would be useless, as there was no way anyone could possibly comprehend what I was feeling. Hell, I barely even understood what was happening to me. No matter how hard I tried, I just could not control it. As I look back now, as I am writing these words, I thank God I never turned to drinking. I found a point where I wanted to turn to alcohol to make this all go away, and I knew that was the time to talk to someone - anyone.

I contacted the veterans help line, and I was referred to a local counselor who specialized in veteran care. I made my first appointment and met with the counselor. I was not sure what I was expecting to get out of this, but I was willing to try. The first meeting was not very productive. I guess you could say it was more of an introduction than a counseling session. The counselor had no military experience, but she claimed to have worked with numerous other patients in similar situations. Above all, she had very promising things to say. I visited her twice a week, and I also sought help from my family doctor. My family doctor prescribed me a medication to help me sleep, and it helped tremendously with the recurring dreams but did little else. Although I was doing this, very few of my problems were actually going away. I was taking all the right steps, but yet I felt like I was getting nowhere.

During one session, I talked about the frustration of not getting better. I explained how I felt as though in some ways it may actually be getting worse.

"Why do you feel as though you're not making progress?" the counselor asked.

I glanced around the room momentarily before answering. The office looked more like a modern living room than an office. I sat on a very comfortable loveseat, while my counselor sat in a typical office-style chair. I loved the way her office smelled. She burned a candle that smelled just like clean laundry fresh from the clothes dryer. I watched the candle's flame dance as I responded.

"Nothing's going away; I'm just not getting anywhere. I just feel like I'm wasting my time here."

She replied, "What are you expecting? Where would you like to see yourself?"

"I'm where I want to be. I don't need to change where I am in life. What I want to change is feeling like shit all the time. Feeling like I have something hanging over me, something stalking me."

I then began to describe to her something new that had recently started. I had been in a local grocery store, and I was doing a quick food shop. As I pushed the shopping cart down an aisle, I suddenly had the strangest feeling that someone was following me. I turned to look behind me, and sure enough, there was no one there. A minute or two later, the feeling returned, but this time it felt overpowering. The aisle felt like it was closing in around me, and I felt like I was in extreme danger. I had an incredible fear come over me for absolutely no rational reason. My heart was racing, and I could barely breathe. I abandoned my groceries, and I went to my car in the parking lot where I rode out this terrifying feeling. It lasted for no more than five or ten minutes, and the feeling vanished as mysteriously as it had appeared. The same episode repeated itself twice again within the same month.

When I finished describing what had happened, I was told I was having panic attacks. She said, "We can get you a mild anti-anxiety medication that should help with that."

I said, "No, no medication. I already take one pill to help me when I'm sleeping, now another one to help me when I'm awake? Then what? Where does it stop? There has to be another way. Aren't you supposed to be able to fix this kind of thing?"

"Bryan, maybe there is another way and maybe there isn't. Either way, I wouldn't know because you hold so much back. You need to open up completely about everything for this to work. You have been coming here for weeks, and you've told me practically nothing. I look at you every time, and I can see you want this to work. I also see that you are trying so hard, but you're also fighting me every step of the way. If you don't open up, we are just not going to get anywhere. I can't make you open up; you have to be willing to trust me."

I was holding back; in fact, I only spoke about a small fraction of the things that had brought me to this point. I admitted this, and I agreed to start being more open and revealing more detail with her. Even though I made that commitment to being more open, it was actually the last time I went to counseling. I cancelled my next appointment and did not return.

As I write this page and I look back, I really cannot explain why I did not return. I think it just goes back to feeling like no one would understand me. I believed then that no matter what I told her, I was going to get the same canned bullshit response that everyone else had been given before me. I knew very little about counseling, and I was not sure what to expect when I went, but I felt like she was merely there to guide me, or advise me on which paths to take to change my way of thinking. I was confused as to how she could guide me on a path she had never walked. The whole thing just stopped making sense to me. I walked away, and I put myself back into the position of trying to figure everything out on my own.

• • •

It was a random Tuesday night when my telephone began to vibrate on the coffee table. I leaned forward just enough to read the caller ID display, "Tony."

Tony was a good friend from the police academy, and he and I had become quite close. However, by this point in time I had not talked to him in weeks, and I could not remember the last time we got together. I contemplated not answering, but I went ahead and picked up.

"Hello."

"Hey man, what's up?" Tony asked.

"Hey buddy! Not a lot, man. What's up with you?"

"Some guys and I are going for wings and beer, want to go?" Tony invited.

"I'm not sure. I have a lot going on tomorrow. Tonight is kind of tough," I replied.

Obviously detecting my answer was half bullshit, Tony said, "No, dude, you're coming. I'll come by your place and pick you up at eight."

I would be lying if I said I actually wanted to go, but I knew I had not been out in a very long time. I answered, "Ok, sounds cool. I'll see you then."

A group of us met at a local bar that was very popular for its chicken wings. Five of us sat around a crowded table, eating our chicken and talking, with the sauce from our wings on our faces. Another friend, Dave, asked me, "You don't seem like yourself lately. Is everything okay?"

"Yeah, I'm fine. I've just been busy lately, and I have a lot on my mind," I told him.

"Is it anything I can help you out with?" Dave asked.

"No, it's nothing big. Just some stupid shit," I told him.

The evening continued on without incident, so I do not really remember much else from that night. The only reason I recall that specific incident is I remember noticing that it was the very first time anyone realized something was wrong. Before that moment, no one had ever asked if I was okay. Maybe I did too good of a job hiding everything to that point, and this was the moment I was not doing such a great job anymore. It could have been that I never did hide anything very well at all, and people were afraid, or felt too awkward, to mention anything. Regardless of the reason, something had obviously changed.

I had spent so long hiding my feelings behind jokes and laughter, to everyone around me that was eventually the person I had become. The jokes and laughter stopped working, and I had abandoned them. Any enjoyment I was once able to have was constantly being interrupted by feelings of extreme guilt. With the smartass façade no longer working, the truth was beginning to reveal itself.

As we ate our wings that night, my mind continually flashed back to starving children, images of Kevin's crippling walk, the thought of a grown man sitting in his urine soaked underwear, and a countless number of other visions of misery. My life had finally reached a point where I enjoyed nothing.

I had completely distanced myself from everyone and everything. I went to work, and I quietly did my job every night. I would then come home and seclude myself to watching television and eating. I stopped caring about my life, I stopped taking care of myself, and I stopped taking care of my relationships. I grew more and more distant from everyone.

My marriage was hanging on by a thread, and I think it was only because I had entirely stopped trying. If I continued to try, it would only have been fight after fight, and I had long since abandoned any expectations. I was tired of being told that she was not attracted to me, and I just opted to not hear anything at all.

For the first time in my life, I found myself alone. I did have people around me, but I had built such a wall around myself, and excluded every person from my life, it was to where I had disconnected from everyone. The exercise equipment in my workout room had not been touched in months, and it showed. My face and body fattened as I filled myself with garbage, and I did little else. The person I used to be was now gone, and I accepted that that this was most likely permanent. I barely recognized the person I had become, inside and out, but I saw no way to change. I saw no way out.

● ● ●

When I first got back from Afghanistan, America was proud of its troops. American flags flew everywhere, "support the troops" stickers were on every other car, and people were quick to shake hands to thank those who fought. I know that people are still proud, but the wars in Iraq and Afghanistan had steadily lost popularity over time. The death tolls began climbing higher and higher, civilian casualties were becoming unacceptable to many, and the very reasons for both wars were being called into question.

No matter what the experience of Afghanistan had done to me, I was always proud that I had been there, proud of what I helped accomplish, and proud of what I had been a part of. I never lost that pride. I was there, and I saw firsthand why we needed to be there. Everyone else on the other hand, they were starting to lose that resolve. Handshakes were being replaced by contempt, and support was being replaced by criticism.

On a random weekend night, I decided to go to a neighborhood restaurant and grab dinner at their bar. The bar, which had a very rustic feel, was in the center of the restaurant. Hardwood planked floors, covered in peanut shells and other debris, gave the restaurant a unique vibe. The bar area was a three sided wraparound bar, with televisions lining the middle. One television was playing a newscast where the anchor announced, "The war in Afghanistan: is it time for America to leave?"

I ate my steak while watching, and the man sitting next to me said, "That shit's turning into another Vietnam."

I said, "You know, in a lot of ways you're right."

"It's an unwinnable war, everyone is just being wasted over there," he declared.

I asked, "How so?"

He told me there was no set mission for Afghanistan, and America was fighting blindly. He described a scenario where America was simply responding to each incident, threat by threat, without ever accomplishing a goal. He said, "And that is a waste of our young men."

"So you think that ousting one of the most dangerous governments on the planet was a waste?" I asked. I continued, "The Taliban posed the single greatest threat to the American people in the last generation. How is that a waste?"

He answered, "Sure, anyone would agree that getting rid of the Taliban was needed, but what have we done since then?"

This guy used the term "we," as if he was somehow a participant in this. I always got a laugh out of people who refer to a sports team as "we," when they clearly don't play for the team. They'll say, "We won the world series," as though the person making that claim had anything to do with the victory. I was beginning to assume that this man had nothing to do with any operations in Afghanistan or the Middle East.

The man continued, "Now we're fighting with insurgents so we can build schools and hospitals for a country that doesn't even want us? That's just stupid. What we need to do is blanket that whole shithole with high explosives, and wipe it off the map."

He looked to be in the age range where he possibly served in Vietnam, and because of his earlier reference to Vietnam, I made the assumption he had been a part of that war. I said, "It's a lot more than that. It's not so simple sometimes, but I'm sure it was the same way when you were in Vietnam."

My assumption turned out to be misguided when he explained he never served. He explained, "No, I wasn't in Vietnam. I was going to go, but it wasn't in the cards for me."

"Were you ever in the military at all?" I asked.

He smugly responded, "No, I went to college so I wouldn't get drafted."

"If you went to college to avoid being drafted, why did you just say you were going to go?"

"Well no, I wasn't going to go to Vietnam. It's just a figure of speech."

"Then why would you say you were going to go, if you weren't?" I asked.

He timidly said, "Look, I'm not looking for a debate or an argument. I was just trying…"

I interrupted, "You were just trying to dump your bullshit opinions on anyone that would listen!"

"Excuse me?"

I said, "Yes, excuse you. You have no idea who I am, but you're going to tell me a bunch of shit about America wasting its men in Afghanistan, and the efforts being useless?" I paused for a moment and asked, "What's my name?"

He asked, "What do you mean, what's your name?"

He and I had not introduced ourselves yet, and we never did. I knew he did not know my name, and I asked again, "What's my name? It's a simple question; just tell me my first name."

"I don't know what your name is."

I calmly explained, "That's right, you have no idea what my name is, because you know nothing about me. You have no idea if I've seen a woman tortured because she wanted to be treated like a human being. You wouldn't know if I had to watch a child die because she wanted to go to school. You wouldn't know. You know nothing about me, but yet you'll sit next to me and tell me what you consider to be a waste. You wouldn't know what a waste actually was if it bit you in the ass."

He said, "I'm sorry. I didn't realize that you... I'm sorry."

He offered to buy me a beer to apologize, and I kindly declined. As he got up from his seat, he said, "I'm just going to move to avoid any awkwardness for you. Again, I'm sorry."

That was just one incident of many. It became commonplace to hear people's opinions on things they knew nothing about. For every one person that would say something positive and kind, two would have diarrhea of the mouth and not know when to shut up.

This change in ideology naturally caused me to question my own beliefs. I began questioning why we were actually fighting these wars. I wanted to believe that the sacrifices I had made and all that I had given was for something. I wanted to believe it was for something greater than me. I truly needed to know that all of this was not for nothing, and I had made a difference, even if in just some small way, to making someone else's life better. News reports and conversations of corporations making billions of dollars off of the war steadily replaced reports of schools for girls, food charities, medical facilities, and the hopes of a better life for the Afghan people.

I struggled with the dilemma of why. Why had I gone to Afghanistan? I thought all along that I really was a part of some greater good, but was it really all for nothing? The conversation with that stranger in the bar replayed itself in my mind, focusing on the thought that this really was a waste. Did I really give up who I was for something that had become nothing more than "a waste?"

It was one thing to deal with everything on its own, but adding the fact that I was now questioning if it was all for nothing made it unbearable. Up until this point, I was able to hold everything together just enough to keep my world from completely falling apart. I now felt like I was becoming exhausted, and I was unable to hold on any longer. Piece by piece, I had fallen apart, and I was ready to let go. I reached the lowest point I had ever been in my entire life, and I was facing this all alone.

• • •

The Boeing 737 airliner rumbled down the runway, building speed as it pressed forward. The engines roared as the front end lifted off the ground, and the aircraft ascended into the air. After a few moments, I was able to release my death grip from the arm rests, and I wiped my sweaty palms on my lap.

"Would you like a drink, sir?" the flight attendant asked as she began taking drink orders.

I always hated flying, and I hoped a drink would take the edge off. I replied, "I'd love a Jack and Coke."

I watched out of the window, as America passed by beneath me. Four and a half hours later, the plane landed safely in Las Vegas. I collected my bag and then took a cab to my hotel. I got myself settled in, and I sent a text message which read, "I'm here. Let me know when you're ready to meet up."

Within a minute, Matt responded, "I'll meet you at the Hard Rock at 5:30, fights start at 6."

I flew to Las Vegas to meet with Matt, an old friend, to watch a mixed martial arts event. Matt still lived in Las Vegas, and he always had great connections for tickets to these events. That night's seats were amazing.

About halfway through the event, Matt began talking with his friend, Charles, who had joined us for a few minutes. Although I had met Charles through Matt before, he proceeded to introduce me again, "Hey Charles, this is my friend Bryan."

Charles said, "Yeah I know Bryan; we've met before." He jokingly continued, "In fact, I'm pretty sure it's you that introduced us the last three times we met."

Matt and Charles then talked while I watched the fight, and I was having a great time. For the first time in a long while, I was actually enjoying myself. Matt said he needed to go talk to another friend for a few minutes and he would be back soon. I did not know Charles very well, but I liked him a lot from what I did know. He was a very sociable and engaging person, and he was very respectful. Charles was a physically big guy, but his personality was even larger. He had a certain presence about him that I can only assume is what made him so successful in business and in life. I do not know exactly how to explain it, other than saying he was just a very comfortable person to be around.

As Matt was leaving, Charles said, "Matt told me you had gone to Afghanistan. I just want to say thank you, and I want you to know that what you did means a lot to me."

I thanked Charles, and after talking for a while longer, he said he wanted me to get with him after the fight. He said, "I want to talk to you about something. So grab me before you leave."

Charles left, and Matt returned a short time later. We laughed and talked as we continued to watch the rest of the event. As we were leaving, I saw Charles and asked, "What did you want to talk about?"

"Oh, hey man! Follow me," he said.

Charles and I walked to a now quiet section of the event center, and we each sat in a seat. Charles said, "I really hope I'm not overstepping any personal boundaries, and I certainly don't want to disrespect you, but I feel like I need to ask you something."

After a brief pause, he continued in a serious tone, "Are you ok?"

I laughed and replied, "Yeah, I'm fine. Why would you ask that?"

Charles said, "I've seen a lot of hurt in my life, and I know what it looks like. There is just something you can see in a person's eyes. No offense, brother, but I am seeing a lot of it when I look at you. I can't walk away from that without asking you if you really are ok."

I insisted to Charles I was fine, to which he replied, "Really? Who are you trying to convince right now, me or you?"

The conversation continued on this way for a few minutes, until I told Charles, "Maybe I'm not fine, but trust me, you wouldn't understand. I don't think anyone would."

At that time, I honestly believed no one could possibly understand anything I was feeling. I think the truth of it was that I was the one who could not understand it. I was the one who was unable to accept the facts as they were. Since I had lost complete control and could not understand or make any kind of sense out of any of this, I assumed no one else possibly could either. Insisting that no one could understand what I was feeling was my last remaining defense mechanism to resist facing the truth of the matter. Everything else had failed, and that was all I had left. I thank God Charles saw through it and pushed me to deal with reality.

"You know what? You're probably right when you say I wouldn't understand, because no matter what it's from, your hurt is different from my hurt, and hell, it's all different from that guy's hurt," Charles said while pointing to a man walking up a staircase. He continued, "It's all different, but at the same time, hurt is hurt. Now, if you don't want to talk to me, you can just tell me to kiss your ass and we'll go our separate ways. I'll hold nothing against you, but if you want to talk, I'll be the first person in the world to listen. I won't judge you, I won't say a word, and I'll just listen."

I said, "Look, you are right. I have a shitload of stuff I would love to let go of, but I don't know how. I don't even know where to begin. It's all very hard to talk about."

Charles told me he understood. He said, "I know it's hard to open up about something, but it's the first step to letting go. Hiding from pain only allows it to grow stronger and stronger. It's like a beast that feeds off of you. It feeds off of you until you actually become the beast."

I asked, "Why are you so concerned about me?" I continued, "Believe me, I'm not trying to be rude, but why do you care so much?"

"Because, I learned something a long time ago: if you try to do only for yourself, you'll only get so far in life. If you reach out to touch other people, you can fix your own soul and move further than you can ever imagine."

Charles then told me a story which brought tears to my eyes. I will never repeat what he told me, but I understood at that point why he was so interested to help me. For the first time in three years, I opened up about everything. I barely knew Charles, but I told him everything I had seen, everything I had felt, and everything I continued to struggle through. I bared my soul, and I told everything to someone who was almost a complete stranger.

As I spoke, Charles barely said a word. He listened intently and offered the occasional head nod to indicate he was following along with the conversation. When I finished I told him, "And now, I don't know what to do next. I feel like none of this is ever going to go away. It just gets worse and worse."

The advice I was given next changed my life forever.

Charles asked, "Are you angry?"

I answered quite certainly, "No."

He said, "I think you are."

"I am? What am I angry about?"

He answered, "You need to figure that out yourself. Hurt, sorrow, sadness, all that shit is easy to let go of. It fades in time on its own. When we lose someone we love, we miss them and it hurts terribly, but it fades. We move forward in life. Anger on the other hand, is like an anchor. It doesn't let you move forward, it holds you right there in one spot. No matter how hard life tries to move you forward, anger keeps you trapped."

"But I'm not angry," I said.

"Have you ever listened to yourself?" Charles asked. He said, "I can hear it in you and it's plain as day. If I tell you what or who you're angry at, it won't be nearly as profound as if you figure it out on your own. You need to look inside and find it. It's right there."

I told Charles I didn't even know I was angry, and I had no idea where to look.

Charles said, "Do you know what you need to do? You need to get a huge stack of paper and just start writing."

"Write about what?" I asked.

"Write about everything, write about anything, or just write about nothing; whatever you want. Write every word you feel, as you're feeling it. Whether it's composed and structured, or just a bunch of words dropping on a page, just write. Put a pen in your hand, and let everything flow through your arm and onto the paper in front of you. Don't do it on a computer, don't type. Just go old school, use a pen and paper. There's something fundamentally soothing about using your own hand to write that allows it to flow more naturally and honestly."

"Ok, I'll try it," I said.

Charles said, "Don't just try it, do it. I write all the time. Usually it's stupid nonsense that wouldn't make sense to anyone else, but to me...to me, it's pure honesty. It allows me to let go of everything. Then I can go back and read it, and I see what's really been hiding from me all along."

Charles looked at me and said, "I believe you can do this. You just need to believe the same thing."

Charles and I spent the better part of the next hour and a half talking about life and reality. I honestly don't know what happened during that time, but Charles made me want to dig deep down within myself and bring out my best again. There was something about that conversation that made me realize not only that I could do this, but I had to. I had no choice but to at least try.

• • •

My Las Vegas weekend ended, and I returned home. The days that followed were filled with recollections of my conversation with Charles, and I could not seem to shake the feeling that it was time to do something about the path my life was taking. Of all the things Charles and I had talked about, two specific parts were called to my attention, over and over again.

I can still hear his words as if they were spoken just yesterday, "If you try to do only for yourself, you'll only get so far in life. If you reach out to touch other people, you can fix your own soul…"

I was also very intrigued by Charles claim that I had anger towards something or *someone*, but I had no idea who. I was interested to learn if I really could identify this, through writing, as he suggested; however, there was also a very significant part of me that was afraid to try any of this. What if I did face my fear, and I could not conquer it? What if I failed at this, as I had at every other step of the way to that point? I felt like this was my last hope, and if this failed, I would have nothing left to hold on to and nothing worth holding on for.

These were the thoughts that invaded my every waking moment for days. Unlike the many other thoughts that had worked their way into my mind over the last three years, these invaders were not unwelcomed. These thoughts offered a glimmer of hope.

Late one night after work, I was in my bed, wide awake, and just staring at the ceiling fan whirling above me. I could only think of my most recent panic attack, which occurred at work earlier that night, and nothing else. After conceding to the fact that I was not going to be able to fall asleep, I found myself in the kitchen with two sleeping pills in my hand. That very moment was when my epiphany came. All of my thoughts, good and bad, collided, and I realized, for the first time, exactly what I needed to do. It was almost is if that magical light switch had finally been turned on. I needed to face my fears, and I knew exactly where I was going to begin.

As I looked at the pills in my hand, I remembered the journal I had written every day while I was in Afghanistan. I realized then that the best way to look towards the future was to have a better understanding of my own past. I knew exactly where the journal was, buried in an old footlocker in the back corner of my garage. I was about to take Charles' advice and begin writing once more, but I knew the place to start was by reviving old memories, no matter how painful they may be. That is how I came to be on the cold cement floor of my garage, reading an old journal into the late hours of the night.

I sat for a long while on the floor, after I finished reading, just letting my entire thought process settle. I started to look inside myself and reflect on who I was, where I was, and how things had become this way. I saw the wall I had built around myself and the barriers I had placed between me and every single person I knew. I clearly saw how I was keeping everyone out, all while holding in everything that was causing so much pain. This could not go on any longer, and it had to come to an end. I had been running from a problem that never went away, and it was never going to go away. I had run so long, I was completely exhausted. For all my running though, I had not even come close to outrunning any of these problems. I had only worn myself down and made them much worse. I was done running, and win or lose, I was ready to fight to get my life back.

● ● ●

Bryan A. Wood

6

Finding Peace

FTER READING MY JOURNAL, I had the immediate urge to begin writing. I had no idea what I was going to write, but I just wanted to start right away. I had no lined paper in the house, so I grabbed a stack of plain, white paper from my computer printer and sat down at the kitchen table. Thankfully, I did not have work the following day, since I was going into my days off. Although it took a little bit to get going, once I started I felt like I could not stop.

I wrote page after page of feelings, emotions, thoughts, ideas, and anything else that came to mind. That first weekend alone, I filled nearly fifty pages with notes, scribbles, and doodles; however, I continued to write at least once a day, every day. Some days, I would only find time for ten minutes, while other days, I would spend up to three hours writing. As time went on, something amazing started to happen. In the beginning, it took a conscious thought for me to write; I had to think about each thought I was going to transfer from my mind to the blank page in front of me. Eventually, I seemed to develop a sort of "autopilot," where I could start writing and just let my mind go as the words just flowed onto the paper.

When I would go into that autopilot mode of writing, I would reflect on the advice given to me to "put a pen in your hand, and let everything flow through your arm and onto the paper." I was doing just that, and it was showing its first signs of success.

Ninety percent of what I wrote during the following two or three weeks was just gibberish and meaningless. The other ten percent though, that proved to be the window I was looking for. I do not think it is entirely necessary to focus too much on what I wrote, as much of it is the basis for the very book you are reading now. There are many things I wrote that I will never share with anyone; those things will always be mine. However, one important line seemed to reveal itself with a regularity that started to bring everything in my life back into focus. I found myself continually writing some variation of, "How could I (*fill in the blank*)?"

"How could I have witnessed death, and then just walked away like nothing happened?" I wrote on one occasion. "How could anyone just go on enjoying anything while knowing that those people are still suffering?" I indicated about myself on another page. "I had a machinegun in my hand, but I did nothing as I watched children, practically still babies, being led away by strangers. How could I have just stood there and done nothing? Fuck orders, I did nothing," I wrote on yet another.

This theme became extremely common, and I realized I was not just angry; I was furious. I was furious at all sorts of things, but most surprisingly, I was angry at myself. I had somehow allowed the sorrow I felt for the things I had seen, to turn into some sort of guilt. That guilt then transformed itself into blame, and it all happened without me ever realizing it. I was blaming myself for everything I had witnessed. I was also viewing every feeling of misery, discomfort, and fear I experienced in Afghanistan as being some sort of punishment, which I was being forced to endure, as a result of that guilt.

I did not look at the fear of rocket attacks and bombings, the humiliation of head lice, the discomfort of mice crawling over me as I tried to sleep, or any countless number of negative experiences as being beyond my control. Instead, I felt as though they were my punishments, the consequences for anything my mind felt I had or had not done. I never, not even once, stopped to process any of these experiences in a healthy, constructive way. I just bottled them away, and I subconsciously justified them to myself as something I deserved, for things that were never my fault.

None of this was ever a conscious thought. I never decided to think that way, and none of it was a choice. It all happened, completely on its own, by trying to ignore everything that I had experienced. I always felt like I would deal with those feelings and emotions when I was ready. The only problem with that rationale is that I never was ready, and I probably never would have been without someone forcing me to confront it.

After weeks of writing, I pored through my piles of paper, and I realized that the last three years were spent punishing myself for something that was never my fault. As I had that very thought, a realization hit me for the very first time: none of this was my fault. I spoke the words out loud, "It's not my fault."

I repeated that phrase over and over again, and I felt a weight being pulled from on top of me. The death, poverty, suffering, abuse, and misery I had seen were not my fault, and I was so very wrong to have ever loaded any of that guilt onto myself.

Although I made this realization, I knew this was only the first step in a very complicated solution. Saying it was not my fault, and truly believing it, was a great step forward, but a feeling like that does not have a light switch, and it could not just be turned off like a glowing bulb. I decided that every day I needed to take small steps towards putting everything back together. It was going to take a constant conscious effort, a lot of self compassion, and a tremendous amount of willpower, but I knew it could be done.

My first step was to make a list of the things I needed to improve in my life, and I prioritized them. The first thing I desperately wanted to work on was myself, on the inside. I knew any lasting improvement to my life needed to be made from the inside out, and not the other way around. I was always looking for some magical answer to come from someone else when all along I was the only one who could start the rebuilding process. This time, I knew I was ready, truly ready, to do what I needed to do.

Within a few days, I scheduled an appointment, and shortly after found myself seated once again in that familiar office, waiting for my counselor to enter the room. She was still using the same scented candle, and the familiar odor of clean laundry was immediately comforting.

She entered the room and enthusiastically announced, "Bryan, I'm so glad you're back."

I started to apologize for giving up and not returning, and she quickly interrupted, "Who cares about that? You weren't ready then, and only you know if you're not ready and more importantly, when you are. Are you ready?"

I replied, "I am." I continued, "But before we get started, I want to give you something. I have something that I want you to see, and that's all I want for today. Next time we'll start talking."

Looking puzzled, she said, "Ok. This isn't normally how we do this, but if it makes you more comfortable, that's fine."

I handed her a pile of papers, a handwritten compilation of my thoughts gathered over the previous weeks. I also handed her my journal, and I told her, "If you read this, I think you'll see exactly where I'm coming from, and we can get started on an even keel. I think you will understand me."

A week later, I returned, and I began to open up in a way that was intimidating, embarrassing, and at the same time absolutely liberating. I went twice a week for several weeks and never missed a session. Some sessions were fraught with sadness, some with anger, and some with fear; however, each was an important step towards finally being free.

A word that came up often in my sessions was the word "free," because it is all I really wanted. I felt like I was being imprisoned by fears and emotions that were crippling at times. I said it many times already, but I was faking every smile, forcing every laugh, and hiding behind every joke. They were all a mask to cover the real emotions to which I had become a slave. They were feelings and memories that were keeping me locked away from who I really was.

I told her about the strange smell from my footlocker that only I could smell. Anyone else to whom I showed the footlocker could not smell a thing, but any time I saw its contents, the odor was so powerful it was like I was still there. I could still smell the Afghanistan air just by looking at the contents of an old box. I told her about the nightmares, the panic attacks, and the horrible memories. I explained how at random moments, while lying in bed, I could still feel mice crawling on me. I knew they were not there, but in that foggy moment between being awake and being asleep, I could feel them. The sensation would snap me fully awake, only to repeat itself time and time again. I described, in detail, the horrible images of death, poverty, beatings, suffering, and fear to which I had bared witness. I shared everything, even my feelings of guilt and blame.

The process of reconciling with myself was not quick, it was not easy, and I cannot pinpoint any one magic moment that made me say: "Aha! This is it." Looking back I can see the progress was steady and consistent, even if it did not always feel that way at the time. The counselor who I had once doubted and swore could never understand me, proved to understand me just fine, and she more than dispelled any doubt I had. She guided me through the process of healing and forgiving myself. She helped me work on issues on the inside and then helped me to establish a plan to begin fixing things on the outside. Moving forward was not accomplished only in the comfort of an ideally scented office alone; it was a constant challenge which I faced every day.

I started off by improving my life alone, focusing on "me." I got back to reading for pleasure again. I always loved learning and reading, and a trip to the local book store kick-started this hobby once again. In no time, I found myself spending hours on the couch reading new and interesting books, learning about life again.

I then examined my lifestyle, and I realized, there is no other way to put it, I was living like shit. I had become lazy, and I was eating horribly. I essentially survived off of soda, frozen dinners, and drive-through restaurants. All of this needed to change. I bought a series of books about nutrition and health, and I navigated my way to a diet plan that worked best for me. I am not going to begin to advocate one health style over another; I just found one that worked for me. I cut out almost all of the meat and dairy in my diet, all of the soda I was drinking was replaced with water, and I began increasing my fruits, vegetables, and alternative sources of protein. I was amazed at how quickly and profoundly this change in diet changed other aspects of my life.

I went to a local sporting goods store and bought a pair of running sneakers. I very reluctantly began running. The first few runs were really more of a hellish jog, but I pushed through. Over time, my pace grew faster and faster, and my distances grew further and further. I stopped filling myself with garbage, and my eating habits did not even resemble what they once were. Within weeks I saw the old me coming back, more and more every day.

On one particular day, I just started jogging. I made a left turn from the end of my driveway and ran. I had no goal in mind, no set destination, and no plan. I felt my heart rate climb, and the sweat began to build on my brow. The air rushed past as I ran faster and pushed further. It was not until about thirty minutes in that I realized I was not tired. I felt like I could go on forever. I looked at the sky, and I listened to the pounding of my feet on the pavement while I thought, "I cannot believe I am actually here." I wanted that feeling to never end. It was during that jog when I decided to go back to another enjoyment in life I had long given up on: training in Jiu Jitsu. Being alive never felt so amazing!

Where my time was once spent eating nothing but processed food and watching television in seclusion, I was now eating right, reading, working out, doing Jiu Jitsu, and always writing. I had come to accept the power of writing, and throughout this process, I never stopped. I knew by then how truly beneficial writing could be, and I have never given up on it.

There were a lot more steps involved in bringing myself to a better place in life, but that really is not the point I want to convey. What I want to get across is that I found a way to identify the true root of all my problems. Even in the face of my own stubbornness, my own reluctance, and my own doubt, I still found a way. Once I did that, I was able to devise a plan to tackle those problems, one by one, until they were all at a manageable level. What was truly amazing was the fact that I only really needed to work on myself, from the inside. I had a plan to start repairing my friendships, my relationships, and my family, but I never needed to move forward with that. Once I had *me* fixed, everything else just seemed to fall in place on its own.

As I mentioned earlier, I have always loved reading. I would just go to a book store, and I would randomly buy a book about a subject in which I knew absolutely nothing. I would start reading until I felt satisfied with the topic and then move on to the next. I started doing this once again, and while shopping online, I found a book about reality and consciousness from a Buddhist point of view. The topic immediately intrigued me, and I started reading everything I could get my hands on.

As I delved deeper into this new topic, I began to truly appreciate the impermanence of life, as well as suffering. Nothing lasts forever, and everything changes. For the good, the bad, and everything in between, everything changes and moves on. I was finally moving on also, and I felt better than I had in years. I accomplished my goal of reaching that small, yet elusive word; I was finally free.

● ● ●

The issues in my marriage continued, and they never seemed to get better. At times there would be moments of brief improvement, but they were usually short-lived at best. There were other issues going on, but this story is not about my marriage, and I refuse to let it become that. One of the things I have learned throughout this entire process is that when you beat yourself up over something internally, you eventually come to accept negativity from outside sources as also being acceptable. After all, if you treat yourself like shit, it must be perfectly fine for others to do the same. That in turn spawns a vicious cycle that continues perpetually unless it is finally broken.

I was looking at myself in the mirror one morning, and I saw the old me, the new me, once again. I stood in front of the mirror for an inordinate amount of time. As I looked at my reflection, I saw a young face looking back. I felt incredibly gifted at that moment, because I realized that one day I would not see the same young face in the mirror; instead, I would be looking at an old man. Sure, that would not be for a long time, but this life really does fly by at a very frightening pace, and in reality, that old man may be looking back at me before I know it.

It made me wonder: what would think of my life, at that moment, the very first time I see myself as an old man. Would I be satisfied, would I have regret, or would I be scared of what was yet to come?

I knew I still had the power at that moment to dictate the course of those answers, and I began to make a series of promises to myself. I promised to never again take a single day for granted. I promised to always strive to be a kinder, gentler, and more understanding person. I promised to enjoy life to its fullest, and make the most of every opportunity and blessing I am given. I promised to stop worrying about the incidental, truly unimportant details we all burden ourselves with on a daily basis. Most importantly, I then promised to never again give my love and affection to anyone who did not purely and honestly deserve it.

Shortly after I made that promise while looking in the mirror, my wife and I had yet another confrontation over our issues. Once again, I was told I was not attractive to her and not loved the way a husband should be loved. The conversation was basically the same as all of the others, with the exception of the major difference that this was the last time I would ever hear her say those words, and this is the last time I will ever refer to her as my wife. I knew I deserved better than what I was being told, and I walked away to find it.

The moment I left, I looked back and wondered how I could have let that go on for so long. I saw life with a clarity that I had lacked before, and it was now painfully obvious what I had missed all along. Not all relationships are meant to last forever, and that is fine. It only becomes a problem when the people in those relationships are not willing to face reality and realize it is simply not right to continue.

It is drilled into us from the day we are born, "If at first you don't succeed, try, try again." While this may be good advice in some scenarios, it usually just places us in a situation where we make the same mistakes over and over, digging ourselves deeper into a hole, while we wonder why things keep going wrong. Sometimes, we need to take a moment to slow down, recognize that whatever it is we are doing just is not working, and move on to a different course of action.

The actual act of leaving my marriage was much more difficult and drawn out than what I am sharing here. I do not go into more detail because I want this story to be about what defines me, and a failed relationship is absolutely not that. While many may consider the final ending of a marriage to be a negative impact on someone's life, in my case it moved me forward in a very positive direction.

● ● ●

After a long, painful, and embattled piece-by-piece reconstruction, my life was finally coming back together. I cannot say I was the same person I was before any of this started, but I was the same person who had since grown, learned, and developed in life. Some things had not gone away, and some still have not to this very day. I still startle very easily, I am still very sad about the life my friend Massoud had endured, and from time to time I can still feel the mice walking across me as I am falling asleep. When I stop and think about her, I can still hear that woman crying over the death of her young child, and I can still feel my stomach drop as I imagine her falling to the ground. I suppose none of those things will ever completely go away, and maybe I do not want them to. They have become part of who I am. These experiences, good or bad, are what makes me the person I have become in life.

The only powerful feeling I felt hanging over me was a need for some sort of redemption. I felt as though I had to do something to truly absolve myself from any remaining guilt that lingered. I continually told myself that those things were not my fault, but it was nearly impossible to completely erase all of that guilt.

I often reminded myself of Charles' words, "If you try to do only for yourself, you'll only get so far in life. If you reach out to touch other people, you can fix your own soul and move further than you can ever imagine," but I never knew exactly how to find the kind of redemption I was searching for. Occasionally in life, the universe will give you a special gift: one that is exactly what you have been praying for, and the first of those precious gifts was to come.

As my life improved in other areas, my life at work excelled also. I never let any of my personal issues invade my work life, although I am sure they may have had some influence on my career. I was very successful at maintaining a barrier between my career and my life beyond work, and it was probably the only figurative wall I built which was actually beneficial. By this time, I was now doing very well at my job, and I was transferred from patrol to a detective position.

In my role as a detective, I initially served in one particular capacity, but I was eventually given the opportunity to expand on that. I was invited to be part of a statewide, multi-agency task force targeting child pornography. The goal of this task force was to identify criminals who were involved in the possession and distribution of this horrific material, and being a part of this team was incredible for me.

Every time an investigation led to the arrest of a pedophile, I would look at them being walked off in handcuffs, and I think to myself, "There is at least one child in this world who will never be hurt because of what happened here today."

The act of watching a child being led off to be raped is an awful thing. Unless you actually live that moment for yourself, it is nearly impossible to understand what it does to your soul. The mental and emotional effect is enormous; it was for me, anyway. I had come to terms with the fact that the things which I had witnessed in Afghanistan were not my fault. Although I did have the physical means to stop them, I did not have the legal means to do so. This was a moral and ethical struggle which took more soul searching than I could ever describe here, but I had eventually come to accept this. Even with acceptance, it is very difficult to let go of a feeling like that. Every time I was a part of the arrest of another pedophile, I was able to let go of a little more. Eventually, I felt as though I had found at least some redemption, and I was honestly never expecting to find that. I knew I somehow still needed to find more, but what I had found to this point was far better than nothing, and it was worth every effort. I was truly free.

• • •

When this story first began, I was watching a beautiful woman's profile being cast by the sun, as it was slowly dipping towards the horizon. Her hair was flowing behind her as she playfully chased a young child. She looked towards me and offered a smile that still melts my soul. She stopped playing and stared at me for a moment. Running her fingers through her hair and smiling, she offered a look that any other man would envy. It was a look of pure love.

"Mommy, keep playing!' the child cried out. The young five-year-old girl looked to me and asked, "Daddy, are you going to play now?"

Without a response, I got up and ran towards her. I picked her up as she leaped up at me saying, "Daddy, it's coming loose again. Will you fix it for me?"

I carried her to a nearby picnic table and set her down. I noticed that the strap to her prosthetic leg was loosening and needed adjustment. I tightened the strap and asked, "Is that better, sweetheart?"

"Thank you, Daddy," she replied as she ran off and continued to play.

The child, a beautiful young girl, played happily although she has just one leg and the other is a prosthetic. She seemed almost unfazed by her disability. This is the moment when I suddenly begin to wake, and in the half confused state between sleep and consciousness, I realized I was simply having this dream yet again. I had the same dream maybe four or five times before, and each time it repeated itself, it became more detailed and vibrant.

Once again, I am certain the universe had blessed me with another special gift: the understanding of how I could truly accept my past, find absolution, and become entirely whole. The advice I was given, "if you reach out to touch other people, you can fix your own soul," made more sense to me than ever. In fact, after years of struggling with what that actually meant, I finally figured it out.

I have believed, ever since I started having this dream, that one day I will save a child, just one, from Afghanistan. That nation is strained with a staggering number of orphans and badly injured children, many of whom are children who will most likely never see adulthood. I have seen their pain, and I have witnessed their horror. I believed at that moment, as I still do to this day, that my mission in life is to save just one child from that existence. Quite wonderfully, I do not share that dream alone.

On a random day, in a random parking lot, I ran into a friend, and I started talking with her. She introduced me to her friend, Abby. Abby was absolutely adorable, beautiful, and a complete smartass. I had a short conversation with my friend, and I drove off wishing I had asked Abby for her phone number. I was far too afraid to just outright ask her, but the feeling must have been mutual. Abby obtained my phone number through our mutual friend, and she sent me a random text message that same night. Before long, we had our first date.

Prior to that first date, Abby and I spent a few days talking on the phone and texting back and forth. She began to tell me about her life, and I told her about mine.

We talked on the phone for hours one night, just talking about our interests, our lives, and just starting to get to know one another. Abby told me about her family and her job, and I told Abby about my friends and my hobbies. We were both dying for that first date to come.

On our first date, we went for a quick dinner before going out for the night. We sat in the restaurant booth, across from one another, and Abby said, "I have something for you."

"For me?" I asked. "You didn't need to get me anything."

Abby fished through her purse and said, "I'll pass it to you under the table." She then leaned forward with her arms obviously extended, and she looked at me with the most adorable smile.

I reached under the table and grasped what I could feel was a DVD case. I asked, "What is this?"

As I brought it up to see what was in my hand, Abby said, "You said you loved *The Simpsons*, and I knew that just came out, so I got it for you."

I looked at what Abby had handed me, and I saw it was the newly released *Simpsons Movie* on DVD. She knew that I enjoyed watching the show, from our earlier conversations, and I had not yet seen the movie. I could not believe she had paid such close attention to everything I told her. My heart began to completely melt, and it has stayed that way ever since. I knew right then and there that she was the one I was always searching for, and now I had found her.

Our first date was a series of minor catastrophes, every plan fell apart, and basically nothing went right. Somehow it did not matter, and we made the best of every minute we had together. Abby and I still refer to it as "the best-worst-date-ever."

That first date turned into a second date, then a third date, and so on, until we fell absolutely in love with each other. Our relationship moved forward at a very steady pace, and I was eternally thankful I was in the right place when I met Abby. I sometimes look back and think to myself: if I had not come so far by the time I met her, Abby and I probably would not have worked. Honestly, we could not have made it together. I would have always felt as if she deserved more or better than what I was. For a long time, I felt that way about everything. With the way things unfolded in the past, I unnecessarily found myself in a state of mind where I honestly believed I was not deserving of any of the gifts life had blessed me with. With Abby, I knew she was exactly where I belonged.

One night, Abby and I were on the couch, talking about our childhoods.

Abby asked, "Tell me something. What is your biggest regret from when you were a kid?"

"That's easy," I said. "Commando. My biggest regret is Commando."

"Be serious!" she said.

"I am being serious. My biggest regret is not beating Commando."

She asked, "Ok, what is Commando?"

"Do you remember the old original Nintendo system?" I asked. I continued, "The problem with it was that you couldn't save your progress. You played the game, but when you shut it off you lost everything, and you needed to start all over the next time you played."

"And what does this have to do with childhood regret?" she asked.

"Well, when I was a kid I loved the game Commando. I played it every day after school and came so close to beating it. For more than a week, I played every day after school until I went to bed. Rather than turn it off and have to start all over again, I put the game on pause and left the Nintendo on. After nine straight days of playing, I was so close to beating the game, but it was time for bed. I left the game on pause and went to sleep, but when I woke up in the morning, my Nintendo was turned off. I went nuts, and I started asking what happened to my game. My mother came in and told me that I left my Nintendo on 'by accident,' so she turned it off for me."

Abby looked at me for a moment like I was crazy before I finished, "I never played the game again. So not beating Commando was my biggest regret."

"You're an idiot," Abby laughingly said.

I did not think much of that conversation at all, until a few weeks later when Abby came to me with a box.

"I have a surprise for you," she said.

I asked, "What's this?"

"Just open it. Come on… Come on… Open it!"

I opened the box, and I saw an original Nintendo system from the 1980s. It had all of the cords and the original controllers.

Abby said, "I found this place online that rebuilds these and makes them like new again. Look inside, there's more."

As I looked through the newspaper that was being used as padding, I found a game cartridge. It was the original Commando.

"Now you can finally beat it," Abby said with a smile.

I set the Nintendo up and started playing the game. It was really not how I remembered it. The game actually fell far short compared to the game systems we are used to playing now, but the effect it had was amazing. Playing that game, for the first time in twenty-some years, reminded me of being eleven again. I was blown away that she did this for me. I was blown away at who I had found.

Time past and over the years since I met Abby, there have been a lot of "Nintendos" between us, metaphorically speaking. It seems like we live our lives for each other, and that makes me happy. That is not to say we do not have little quarrels and spats like everyone does. We argue sometimes if I do not clean up after myself or if she spends too much money at the mall, but we never lose focus on what really matters. From the moment I met her, I have never gone a single day where I did not feel loved, and that is truly more important to me than anything. It is a feeling I think is lost or abandoned on many other people.

Abby and I moved into a beautiful home, and together we have built a wonderful life; it is a life of happiness, love, and enjoyment. It has been an easy road at times and a bumpy road at others, but I would not trade a moment of it for the world.

Since the first day I started writing, so long ago, I have made extraordinary improvements in my life. I took them day by day, and they were so minor at times, it was difficult to actually notice the changes as they happened. However, looking back over time evokes a feeling of amazement in myself at what I accomplished. It is difficult to pinpoint exactly when I felt "whole" again, but it was at some point after meeting Abby. With her, the few remaining holes I had left were completely filled in. The guilt, remorse, and sadness are never completely gone, but they do not interfere with my life at all. The panic attacks, recurring nightmares, and fear, on the other hand, they are gone; none of them have ever returned, but I would be lying if I said I didn't absolutely hate mice to this very day. I am fairly certain I always will.

I do not think Abby realizes it, but each and every day I look at her and realize she is the reason I am who I am. It just does not get any simpler than that.

• • •

After I returned from Afghanistan, I built an impenetrable fortress around myself, and I blocked out nearly all of my old friends. Very sadly, most of these friendships never really grew back. The time that passed, between the walls I had put up and when I was ready to take them back down, was enough that most people's lives had moved on, and they had gone in very different directions. I tried to rekindle some old friendships on a few occasions, but I think just too much time had passed.

Although the old friendships may have long since expired, I have opened up to new people, and I have a very close group of friends I have welcomed into my life. Rather than shutting people out, I am welcoming new people in. Admittedly, it is easier to make friends with people who have been through war or some other similar experience because I still have that feeling that someone who has been through something like that has an understanding of me that very few ever will. I suppose that will never change, and I really do not want it to. With that thought in mind however, I do limit the number of friends who have had those same experiences so I don't confine myself to just that. It was a mistake I made in the past, to surround myself only with "people like me," thinking it would make things better or somehow easier. I know I need to be realistic; that has never worked out very well in the past, so there is no need to repeat the same behavior again.

My professional life has continued to advance as well, and I no longer work in the capacity where I was when I was with the child pornography task force. I am glad I had the opportunity to serve such a noble cause, but I am also glad I will never do that kind of work again. There are some things in life that you can never un-see, and that job was filled with them. I will always be grateful that life gave me the opportunity to do that, because, in an indescribable way, it helped set me free.

I now have been given the opportunity to work a quiet desk job, and it is actually one that does not require me to regularly carry a gun. A lot of people may consider what I do to be somewhat boring, but boring is exactly what I enjoy now. I think I have seen more than my share in life, and I am ready to let the next guy take his turn. There is an old saying that one who lives by the sword will likely die by the sword, and I have lived by the proverbial sword more than enough for one lifetime.

● ● ●

On a random Tuesday not very long ago, Abby and I were getting ready for work. Abby was sleeping late, as usual, and she did not want to get out of bed.

"If you're not out of bed in one minute, I'm coming in there to tickle you," I told her.

"Okay, Okay, I'm up," Abby replied as she got out of bed.

"Too late," I said as I ran up to her. I continued, "You're getting tickled anyway."

Abby and I tickled and laughed for a few minutes, and we then began getting ready for work. It was a beautiful day, and nothing was unusual in the least. We played and goofed around as we got ready for work, just as we do every other day.

"Babe, don't forget it's trash day," Abby reminded me.

"Ok, I'll do it right now."

I removed the trash bag from the waste can in the kitchen, and I tied the top of the bag into a knot as I walked to the garage. Once in the garage, I placed the bag into the trash barrel and began dragging it to the curb.

I was roughly half way to the curb when my left leg had a bizarre sensation, and I could not move it. The sensation lasted for only a moment and immediately subsided. Within a step, my right leg felt a similar sensation, and I suddenly had to struggle to move either leg. I fell to the ground spilling the trash, and I needed to grab the bumper of my car to get back to my feet. I was having the hardest time standing, and I was very confused. I was young, healthy, and had no medical problems; I couldn't understand what was happening to me.

Getting back into the house was a struggle. My mind raced trying to figure out what was happening, but I knew that I needed to get into the house, to Abby, so she could call for help. Otherwise, it could be ten minutes or more before she noticed I had not come back inside. I managed to make my way from the garage into the laundry room, and I stumbled through the kitchen, where I fell to the living room floor. By this point, I could not feel my legs, and I could slowly feel I was losing all feeling throughout my body. I tried to speak, but I could not utter a word. I had the most bizarre sensation in my head, and I thought I was about to die. The single question, "Is this really how I am going to die?" ran through my head.

Abby called 9-1-1, and I was taken to the emergency room, where I started to feel better over the course of several hours. The staff in the hospital was mystified as to what had happened, and they offered no positive explanations. After a few days, I felt much better but there were a lot of lingering effects that took months to completely vanish. Some of these were subtle and unnoticeable to others, while others were not so discrete. For months, I would stumble on my words, I was constantly dropping things, and I had the coordination of a three legged rocking horse. Eventually, these lingering problems went away completely, and over time I would ultimately find out what had happened to me.

It is funny how you can look back at previous problems in life and realize they were never really as bad as you had made them out to be, especially when compared to a real problem. You look at something that was once the worst thing to have ever happened in your life, and then something else comes along and becomes the new reigning champion.

The result of what happened to me that day does not affect me today, it probably will not affect me tomorrow, and it should not affect me any time soon, but one day it could alter my life in every way imaginable. I face the reality that at some point in my life I may be in a wheel chair because of this, and the things I take for granted today may one day just be a fond memory. I pray that day never comes, but the statistical reality is that it will. Throughout it all, Abby has promised to be there every step of the way, and she has vowed, "I will always be right here with you, no matter what." I am going to tell you right now, if that is not love then I don't know what the hell love is. Isn't that something? I found my angel.

● ● ●

Life is a funny thing. Just when you clean up one pile of shit, another dog comes along to leave you a fresh, steaming new one. I know now, that at the end of the day, it is all what *you* make of it. I said it at the very beginning: you will certainly face challenges in your life, but it is how you face and overcome these challenges that will ultimately define you as a person. Believe me, there was a time when I did not understand what that meant, but I do now. Holy shit, I do now.

No matter what life brings to me, I know I will always find a way to get by. I, like everyone else, have no way of knowing what tomorrow is going to bring, but I do know I will always have the strength to get through it. I will never quit, I will never surrender, and I will always prevail.

Any time I find myself feeling as though I am in over my head, my mind is always able to retreat to one comforting thought. I picture myself all alone, behind a machine gun, in the middle of Afghanistan. I picture myself along the wall of the Camp Eagle compound, late at night, writing in my journal by moonlight, and it always brings back one vivid memory which I hope to never lose.

I remember being on the wall overlooking the city street, writing away, and stopping to gaze up at the starry sky. Being in a place where I am surrounded by poverty and violence, all I needed to do was look up to see an endless beauty in the night's sky. I remember the darkness of Kabul made the stars shine brighter than I had ever seen, or have seen since. All I need to do is think about it for a moment, and I can feel the cool mountain air against my skin, bringing with it the feeling that even within the worst, there is always something worth finding. Amongst the violence, I had found peace.

I can still picture myself as that kid, writing in the middle of the night in Afghanistan, having no idea what life was going to bring. Then I look at myself now, and I realize how much my life has changed since those days. I am still completely unaware of what life has in store for me next, but this time, no matter where life's next journey may lead, I will always have the strength and courage to never again feel the crippling pain of my own unspoken abandonment.

The End

● ● ●

Made in the USA
Lexington, KY
10 June 2013